50 FAT QUARTER MAKES

FIFTY SEWING PROJECTS MADE USING FAT QUARTERS

Edited by Ame Verso

D&C

David and Charles

www.stitchcraftcreate.co.uk

----CONTENTS----

50 FAT QUARTER MAKES

----INTRODUCTION----

Every crafter just loves to stash fabric – especially fat quarters – and is always on the lookout for new ideas to quilt, stitch and appliqué. *50 Fat Quarter Makes*, brought to you by eleven talented designers, is overflowing with exciting and inspirational projects for all those lovely fabric bundles: the ones you already have stored away and those you are yet to buy!

So what exactly is a fat quarter? Taken from one yard of fabric, fat quarters are cut in half lengthways and then in half widthways to form a quarter cut, (usually) measuring 18 × 22in (46 × 56cm). Widely available pre-cut in an array of patterns and colours; their squarer shape makes them highly versatile for patchwork, appliqué, strip piecing and more, which is why crafters adore them so much.

This unique collection begins with single fat quarter patterns for everyday items, such as pincushions and purses, that can be completed in less than a day. You can then move onto more complex projects requiring a small handful of fat quarters: from a fun girly twirly skirt to a lovely sewing machine cover, and even a decorative family of fabric hedgehogs to brighten up your home. If you are feeling ambitious, why not savour the stunning projects that use up to ten fat quarters? They will bust your much-loved fabric stash and give you family heirlooms to treasure, including beautiful quilts, striking pillows and a delightful reversible table runner that will take you from winter through to summer. The handy side bar on every page will tell you at a glance how many fat quarters you will need for each project – just look for the shaded diamonds.

So be inspired, release that fabric stash and get creative with these easy-to-follow patterns, complete with a handy stitch library to get you started. Everything you need in one beautiful package to make a wealth of useful and stylish projects for your home, garden, family and friends, and even your pets.

----LITTLE MOUSE PINCUSHION----

Jessie Fincham

This cute and charming mouse is the perfect home for all your pins. Surprisingly simple to create using a fat quarter of your favourite fabric and the templates provided, it will certainly add character to your sewing supplies.

MATERIALS

- 1 fat quarter of fabric
- Scrap of cardboard
- Scrap of white felt
- Black embroidery cotton (floss)

1 Using the templates provided (see Templates), cut one of the following from the fat quarter: sides A and B, head and base. Now cut another base from cardboard and two ears from white felt.

2 Fold the ears slightly to bunch in the middle and tack (baste) them in position between the marks on the head.

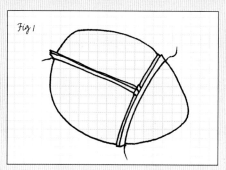

Fig 1

3 Sew the sides together along the long, unnotched edge. Then sew the short edge of the side section to the head (see Fig 1).

4 Using black embroidery cotton (floss), sew two French knots for the eyes. To make the tail, knot the end of the cotton and sew from the inside of the back of the mouse to the outside. Secure with a knot at the base of the fabric and trim. Repeat with a couple of lengths of embroidery cotton to form the whiskers.

5 Stitch the body to the fabric base, matching the notches and leaving an opening for the stuffing. Turn right side out.

6 Trim the cardboard template by ¼in (6mm) and insert it through the opening. Fill the mouse tightly with toy stuffing and whipstitch the gap to close.

----FUNKY MUG RUG----

Cynthia Shaffer

This vibrant coaster panel, formed from a single fat quarter, is guaranteed to brighten up your coffee table. Make the most of your print by fussy cutting the panels, quilting in contrasting thread and adding cute button details.

MATERIALS

- 1 fat quarter of large print fabric
- 1 sheet of vellum
- 10 × 7in (25 × 18cm) thin wadding (batting)
- 36in (91.5cm) double fold binding
- 4 small buttons

◆ PATTERN NOTES

Seam allowance is ¼in (6mm)

1 Cut a 4¾ × 5½in (12 × 14cm) rectangle from the fat quarter. Fussy cut to centre the yellow medallion.

2 Draw a 3¼ × 2¾in (8 × 7cm) rectangle. Using a pair of compasses, add a quarter circle with a 2½in (6.5cm) radius at the bottom left corner of the rectangle. Trace this template onto the vellum and transfer the quarter circle.

3 Cut the template four times from the fat quarter, following the quarter circle shape to fussy cut these panels. Cut two panels with the template facing up and two facing down.

4 Stitch the four panels together, then stitch to the panel from Step 1.

5 Cut a 10 × 7in (25 × 18cm) panel from the fat quarter. Position face down, then place the wadding and the pieced panel on top. Pin and machine quilt the layers together using contrasting thread. Stitch circles around the yellow medallion, then stitch around the pieced panel, following the semi circles and sewing in the ditch.

6 Stitch the binding to the outer edge and attach the buttons, as shown.

----CHIC SUNGLASSES CASE----

Ali Burdon

This stylish case, sewn from a single fat quarter, is perfect for protecting your summer shades. The button and loop fastening gives you easy access to your eyewear and you can mix and match your styles by experimenting with different fabrics and trims.

MATERIALS

- 1 fat quarter of fabric
- 10in (25cm) medium loft fusible fleece
- 10in (25cm) medium weight iron-on interfacing
- 2in (5cm) length of ribbon, lace or trim
- 3in (7.5cm) length of elastic cord
- ¾in (2cm) diameter button

◆ PATTERN NOTES

Seam allowance is ¼in (6mm)

1 Cut four pieces from the fat quarter (two for the outer and two for the lining), two pieces from the fusible fleece and two pieces from the interfacing, each measuring 6 × 8in (15 × 20cm). Iron the fusible fleece to the outer fabric and the interfacing to the lining fabric, following the manufacturer's instructions.

2 Fold or trim the ribbon in half and pin, right sides together, 2¾in (7cm) from the top right-hand edge of the outer front. The raw edges of the ribbon should just overlap the right-hand raw edge of the fabric.

3 Place the second piece of outer fabric right sides together with the first, sandwiching the folded ribbon in-between. Pin and stitch the sides and bottom seam. Pin the lining fabrics, right sides together, then stitch the side and bottom seams, leaving a 3in (7.5cm) opening in the centre of the bottom seam for turning.

4 To create the flat base, draw a 1in (2.5cm) square at each bottom corner of the lining section. Open out the pouch and pinch one of the corners, bringing the side and bottom seams together. Match the markings and then stitch along the line created, reverse stitching at both ends. Repeat for the other corner. Trim the excess fabric at the corners, leaving a ¼in (6mm) seam allowance, then turn right sides out and iron. Repeat for the outer section pieces.

5 Mark the mid-point of the lining on the top edge of the back section. Fold the elastic cord in half and tack (baste) the loop within the seam allowance at this point on the right side of the lining. The raw edges of the loop should just overlap the raw edge of the lining, and the loop itself should point towards the lower seam.

6 Turn the outer section right sides out and place it into the lining section, right sides together. The loop should be sandwiched between the lining and the outer, with just the raw edges showing. Line up the side seams, pin around the top edge and stitch.

7 Turn the pouch through the opening. Iron the top seam and topstitch it close to the edge. Fold the top down and stitch the button in place. Finally, ladder stitch the gap in the lining closed.

JUST FOR YOU GIFT BAG

Jo Avery

This gorgeous gift bag with pretty ribbon ties is given a truly personal finishing touch with the recipient's initial sewn on with buttons. As an alternative, use a fat quarter of festive fabric and red ribbon to make the cutest gift bag for Christmas.

MATERIALS

- 1 fat quarter of fabric
- 2yd (1.8m) of ribbon
- 15–20 small buttons

1 Cut a strip from the bottom of the fat quarter so the remainder measures 15in (38cm). Cut the strip in half to make two 10¾ × 15in (26.5 × 38cm) rectangles.

2 To mark the opening for the tie, make a small pencil line 6½in (16.5cm) from the short side in the seam allowance on the wrong side of the fabric. Draw another line ¾in (2cm) above this and repeat on the opposite side.

3 Pin the two pieces of fabric right sides together. Using a ½in (1.2cm) seam, sew along the two long sides and the bottom, leaving the opening.

4 Trim the threads at the opening, clip the bottom corners and iron the seams open. Turn inside out and push out the corners with a wooden stick or similar.

5 Draw a 2½in (6.5cm) tall initial, 1in (2.5cm) from the bottom, and sew the buttons in place.

6 Draw two parallel lines between the openings on each side on the right side of the front and back. Open out the bag, turn over a ½in (1.2cm) seam at the top and turn over again so the folded edge sits ¼in (6mm) below the bottom of the opening. Pin from the right-hand side and repeat with the opposite opened-out seam. Now pin the same folded edge in line around the right side. Straight stitch around the bottom marked line, catching the folded top edge in the seam. Repeat with a parallel line around the top of the opening.

7 Cut the ribbon in half. Attach a safety pin at the end of one piece of ribbon and feed it all the way around, so it comes out at the opening it started from. Repeat with the other ribbon half in the opposite opening. Pull the ribbon sides together to gather and knot at each side.

----CHARMING COIN PURSE----

Kaye Prince

Featuring a strong faux leather base panel and zip fastening, this coin purse is both pretty and practical. As it uses just one fat quarter, there is nothing stopping you from making a variety of purses in different colourways to complement your every look.

MATERIALS

- 1 fat quarter of fabric
- 1 fat quarter of medium weight interfacing
- Small piece of faux leather
- 7in (18cm) zip

◆ PATTERN NOTES

Seam allowance is ½in (1.2cm)

Top Tip

FOR NEAT ZIP CORNERS, FOLD THE TABS TOWARDS THE OUTER PIECES AND THE SEAMS TOWARDS THE LINING PIECES.

1 Cut four 5 × 6in (13 × 15cm) rectangles (two for the outer and two for the lining) and two 1¼ × 2½in (3 × 6.5cm) rectangles (for zip tabs) from the fat quarter. Cut a ¾ × 2½in (2 × 6.5cm) and two 6 × 1½in (15 × 4cm) rectangles from the faux leather and two 5 × 6in (13 × 15cm) rectangles from the interfacing.

2 Fuse the interfacing to the outer pieces, following the manufacturer's instructions. Align a leather piece along the bottom edge of an outer piece and topstitch along the top edge of the leather. Repeat for the other outer piece.

3 Evenly trim the zip to 5½in (14cm). Take one zip tab piece, iron each short edge in towards the wrong side by ¼in (6mm) and fold in half widthways. Repeat. Fit the zip end inside the tab, butting the end up against the fold, and topstitch in place across the ironed edge. Repeat at the other end of the zip with the second tab.

4 Centre and place the zip, face down, along the top edge of the right side of one outer panel. Place one lining panel right side down on top and pin. Stitch through all three layers using your zipper foot. Turn the panel right side out so the lining and outer pieces are wrong sides together and iron. Repeat for the second outer piece, placing it right side up and laying the sewn piece on top with the zip side down. Topstitch the fabric together along each zip edge.

5 Fold the small leather rectangle in half widthways. Align and iron the raw edges along one side of an outer piece, about 1in (2.5cm) from the zip. Tack (baste) in place.

6 Open the zip at least three-quarters of the way and fold the purse so both lining and outer pieces are aligned right sides together. Stitch around the purse, leaving a turning gap in the bottom of the lining. Turn right sides out, using a wooden stick or similar to push out the corners. Stitch the opening closed and iron.

---DAPPER DOG BANDANA---

Louise Horler

Ensure your pooch is the coolest in the park with this trendy bandana, simply made from a fat quarter of the most stylish fabric. For a professional finish, the bandana can be fastened with poppers that are sewn or hammered in place.

MATERIALS

- ◆ 1 fat quarter of cotton fabric
- ◆ 1 fat quarter of fleece or towelling fabric
- ◆ Fastening of your choice such as poppers (snaps)

◆ PATTERN NOTES

Seam allowance is ⅜in (1cm)

1 Using the pattern (see Templates), cut one triangle from the cotton fabric and one from the fleece or towelling fabric.
2 Lay the fabric piece pattern side up and the fleece piece face down on top. Pin around, leaving a 2½in (6.5cm) turning gap halfway along the right hand side.
3 Machine stitch around the fabric triangle, leaving the gap open, then clip the corners. Turn the bandana through to the right sides, push out the corners with your fingers and then iron.

4 Topstitch close to the edge all around the bandana, closing the turning gap.
5 Add a fastening at the back: you can use poppers hammered in position, sew-on poppers or a hook-and-loop fastening.

Top Tip

MAKE SURE YOU SEW SEVERAL REINFORCING STITCHES AT THE START AND FINISH OF YOUR SEWING.

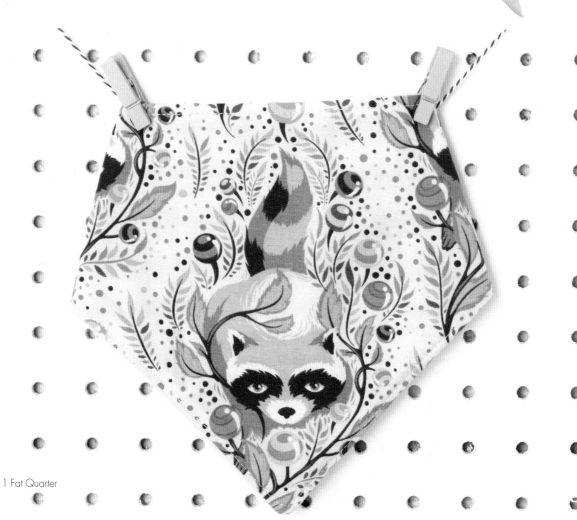

---HEXY GARLAND NOTEBOOK HOLDER----

Jo Avery

This stylish notebook holder is a great gift for a student. The instructions are to fit an A5 notebook: to make a different size simply measure your notebook and add ½in (1.2cm) all the way around, including the depth of the spine.

MATERIALS

- 2 fat quarters of fabric: main and lining
- 1½ yd (1.4m) length of ribbon
- Paper

1 Cut a 12¾ x 9¼in (32.5 x 23.5cm) rectangle from both the main and lining fabrics. Cut two 8½ x 9¼in (22 x 23.5cm) rectangles from the lining fabric. Cut the ribbon into one 18in (46cm) and one 22in (55cm) lengths.

2 Cut six hexagons from the lining fabric using the fabric template (see Templates) and six paper hexagons using the paper template. Pin a paper hexagon centrally onto the wrong side of a fabric hexagon and fold the fabric edges over the paper. Tack (baste) through the paper to secure. Repeat for all six hexagons.

3 With right sides facing, whipstitch two hexagons together, just catching the edge of the seam without sewing through the paper. Sew each seam separately to form a hexagon garland, as shown in the photograph. Iron both sides and remove the papers.

4 Fold the main fabric in half, wrong sides together, iron and unfold. Pin the hexagon garland 1in (2.5cm) from the top edge, centred between the ironed line and right-hand edge, then slipstitch in place.

5 Fold two smaller lining fabric pieces in half on the shorter side, wrong sides together, and iron to make pocket pieces.

6 Layer the fabric pieces from the bottom up as follows: lining (right side up); line up the raw edges of the pockets with the lining edges and folds towards the centre on both sides; main piece (right side down). Pin around, leaving a central 3in (7.5cm) turning gap in the bottom edge.

7 Insert the shorter ribbon into the seam so the raw edges poke out slightly, positioning it ½in (2.5cm) below the centre. Place the longer length on top, between the main and pocket pieces on the back cover. Pin the ribbons in place between the seams, ensuring the bulk is in the centre of the fabric sandwich, away from the seams.

8 Sew around, leaving the 3in (7.5cm) turning gap. Snip the corners, turn right sides out and iron. Turn under the seams and hand sew the gap closed with invisible slipstitches or ladder stitch. Insert the notebook, wrap the ribbon around and tie in a bow at the front.

----GIRLY TWIRLY SKIRT----

Emily Levey

This gorgeous gathered skirt features an elasticated waistband for comfort, and a contrasting hem band for style. By cutting the elastic to size, the skirt can be made to fit girls of three to six years. A larger skirt can be sewn for an older child by increasing the size of the contrasting hem band, however it will not be as full.

MATERIALS

- ◆ 2 fat quarters of fabric: main and accent
- ◆ ¾in (2cm) wide elastic, cut to child's measurements

◆ PATTERN NOTES
Seam allowance is ⅝in (1.5cm)

1 Cut selvedges of the same size from the fat quarters. Cut your main print fat quarter in half along the length, as shown (see Fig 1).
2 With right sides facing, join the two halves along the short edge to give you a 10 × 44in (25 × 112cm) rectangle. Finish the seam allowance and iron.
3 Cut two rectangles from the accent fabric measuring 5½in (14cm) × width of fabric (see Fig 2).
4 With right sides facing, join the two halves along the short edge to form a 5½ × 44in (14 × 112cm) rectangle. Finish the seam allowance and iron.
5 With right sides facing, join the two skirt panels along the long edge (see Fig 3), finish the seam and iron downwards. If you are using a directional print, ensure the accent fabric is sewn along the bottom edge.
6 Join the sides of the skirt to form a tube, finish the seam and iron. Ensure the seam on the hem band matches up on each side.
7 Turn over the top edge of the skirt by ¼in (6mm), bringing the raw edge over to the wrong side of the fabric, and iron. Now turn over by 1in (2.5cm), enclosing the raw edge, and iron again. Stitch around the top of the skirt, ⅞in (2.2cm) from the top edge, to catch this fold. Leave a 2in (5cm) gap for inserting the elastic.

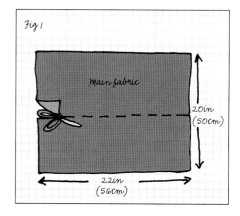

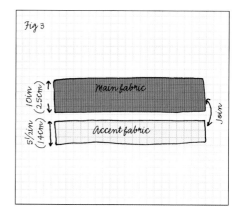

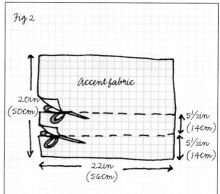

8 To make the hem turn over the bottom edge by ¼in (6mm), bringing the raw edge over to the wrong side of the fabric, and iron. Turn over again by 1in (2.5cm), enclosing the raw edge, and iron. Stitch around the bottom of the skirt, ⅞in (2.2cm) from the bottom edge.

9 Cut a length of elastic to the child's measurements, using the following as a guide:

3 years = 18¾in (48cm)

4 years = 20in (50cm)

5 years = 21in (53cm)

6 years = 22in (56cm)

10 Using a large safety pin, feed the elastic around the skirt in the top opening, taking care not to twist it. Overlap the ends by 1in (2.5cm) and secure together with a zigzag stitch. Stitch the opening closed.

11 Topstitch around the top of the skirt twice, sewing through the elastic to prevent it from twisting whilst being worn (see Fig 4). Stretch out the elastic as you sew to ensure that the fabric lies flat.

Top Tip

IF THE ELASTIC IS SLACK, A GENTLE STEAM WITH AN IRON ON A HIGH STEAM SETTING WILL HELP IT TO SHRINK BACK. HOLD THE IRON JUST ABOVE THE FABRIC WITHOUT TOUCHING IT.

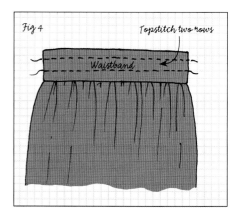

Fig 4 — Topstitch two rows — Waistband

----CURIOUS CAT DOORSTOP----

Lisa Fordham

This charming doorstop is simple to sew from just two fat quarters using the templates provided. The addition of a filled beanbag inside the body makes the doorstop fully functional, as well as adding bags of character to your home.

MATERIALS

- ◆ 2 fat quarters of fabric
- ◆ 1kg (2lb 4oz) of dried beans
- ◆ 2 small black buttons
- ◆ Toy stuffing

◆ PATTERN NOTES
Seam allowance is ⅛in (4mm)

1 Using the templates provided (see Templates) cut the following from the two fat quarters: one bottom panel, two body pieces, two head pieces, four ears, four paws, two tails and two beanbag pieces.

2 With right sides facing, machine stitch two ear shapes together, leaving a turning gap, and turn right sides out. Lightly stuff with toy stuffing, fold in by ⅛in (4mm) and hand stitch the gap closed. Repeat for the other ear, the tail and the two paws.

3 With right sides facing, pin and mark areas on the head to be left open for the ears and neck. Leave a 2¼in (5.5cm) opening for each ear, with a 2¾in (7cm) gap between them. Machine stitch the head pieces together around the openings and turn the head right sides out. Place the stuffed ears into each opening and hand stitch them in position on both sides. Lightly stuff the head with stuffing, being careful not to overfill, then hand stitch the opening in the neck closed.

4 With right sides facing, stitch the bottom panel to the base of the each body piece. Machine stitch around the body, leaving a gap for stuffing and inserting the beanbag on one side.

5 Machine stitch the two beanbag pieces together, leaving a small gap. Insert the beans through the opening then machine stitch it closed. Fill the body with stuffing, inserting the beanbag last, then add just a small amount of stuffing to finish. Fold down the small seam around the bottom piece and hand stitch in place.

6 Stitch claw lines onto the paws with black wool and stitch the paws and tail in position. Make the face by attaching two black buttons for the eyes and backstitching a nose and whiskers using black wool. Finally, stitch the head to the front of the body.

----SILHOUETTE PETS CUSHION----

Jessie Fincham

Whether you love cats or dogs, this simple double-sided cushion cover is sure to delight. Find a striking silhouette of a dachshund sporting a fancy neckerchief on one side or turn over for an elegant feline friend, complete with cute ribbon collar.

MATERIALS

- ◆ 2 fat quarters of fabric
- ◆ Scraps of black felt
- ◆ Scraps of fabric and ribbon
- ◆ 12in (30cm) zip

1 Cut a 17in (43cm) square from both fat quarters for the cushion sections.

2 Using a crayon, transfer the dog and cat (see Templates) onto black felt and cut out. Transfer the neckerchief template onto the fabric scrap, cut out and secure to the felt dog using straight stitch. Tie a ribbon bow around the cat and trim the ends.

3 Find the centre of the cushion by folding diagonally, then diagonally again. Pin the cat to the centre and sew around, 3mm (1/8in) from the edge. Repeat for the dog on the other fat quarter square.

4 With right sides facing and using a longer stitch length, sew along one side of the cushion, 1in (2.5in) from the edge. Iron the seam open.

5 Pin the zip in place on the central seam, with it facing up towards the seam. Using a zipper foot, sew a straight line at either side of the zip, carefully guiding it to correctly align. Turn and sew the sides of the zip to box it in (see Fig 1).

6 Use a seam ripper to remove the stitches from the central seam. This will expose the zip. With the zip at least half open, continue to sew the remaining three sides, using a 1in (2.5cm) seam allowance. Trim the corners, sew a zigzag stitch to prevent any fraying, and then trim the edges further using pinking shears.

7 Turn the cushion right sides out, using a wooden stick or similar to push out the corners.

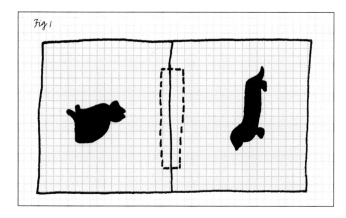

Fig 1

----DITSY TEDDY BEAR----

Prudence Rogers

This little floral bear is so sweet on her own, but she wouldn't be seen without her miniature dress. It only takes two fat quarters, but you can have fun using up fabric scraps to make her a whole wardrobe!

MATERIALS

- 2 fat quarters of fabric: main teddy and dress
- 28in (71cm) length of ¼in (6mm) wide ribbon
- Toy stuffing

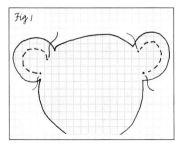

Top Tip

THE HEM IS A LITTLE TRICKY TO SEW, DUE TO THE SIZE OF THE DRESS. IT HELPS TO TURN THE DRESS TO RIGHT SIDES, WHILE STILL SEWING THE HEM FROM THE WRONG SIDE.

1 Using the template (see Templates), cut out two teddy shapes from the main fabric (seam allowance is included).

2 Place the teddy bear's right sides facing and sew around, using a ¼in (6mm) seam allowance and leaving a 2in (5cm) turning gap down the outer side of one leg.

3 Cut into the corners and clip all the curves on the seam allowance. Turn to right sides through the opening and iron.

4 Sew ¼in (6mm) from the edge around each ear through both thicknesses of fabric (see Fig 1).

5 Stuff the teddy with toy stuffing through the opening in the leg. Fold the raw edges of the opening under to match the seams and slipstitch closed by hand.

6 Hand sew the eyes, nose and mouth using satin stitch and backstitch in a contrasting colour, as shown in the photograph.

7 Cut two dress shapes (see Templates) from the second fat quarter. With right sides up, fold over each armhole by ¼in (6mm) around the curve and iron. Don't worry if the

seam allowance becomes smaller as the turn tightens. Stitch the folded edge around each armhole closed (see Fig 2).

8 Fold the top neckline down by ¼in (6mm), then a further ⅜in (1cm) to conceal the raw edge, then iron and pin. Sew close to the bottom folded edge to make a casing for the ribbon. Repeat for the other dress piece.

9 With right sides facing, pin the front and back dress pieces together. Sew down each straight side using a ¼in (6mm) seam allowance. Finish the seam with zigzag stitch and fold to one side (see Fig 3).

10 Fold and iron a ⅜in (1cm) hem around the bottom of the dress and sew ¼in (6mm) from the folded edge.

11 Thread a 14in (35.5cm) length of ribbon through each casing, using a small safety pin at one end. Centre the ribbon and sew a small vertical row of stitching in the middle of the casing. Heat-seal the ends of the ribbon to prevent them from fraying. Place the teddy in the dress, pull up the ribbons to gather the top and tie in a bow at each side.

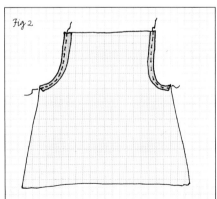

Fig 1

Fig 2

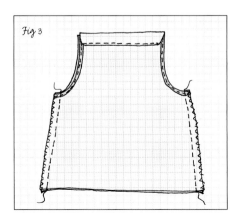

Fig 3

----CUTE COLLAR BIB----

Jessie Fincham

This baby bib is both pretty and practical with its unique collar detail and simple ties. I chose a delightful washday patterned fabric with contrasting pink for the binding and ties. To suit a baby boy, try substituting with navy blue and white fat quarters for a cute sailor theme.

MATERIALS

- ◆ 2 fat quarter of fabric: main and binding
- ◆ 11 × 9in (28 × 23cm) scrap of wadding (batting)

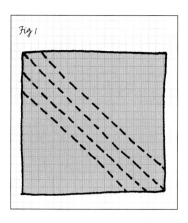

Fig 1

1 Using the templates provided (see Templates) cut two bib shapes from the main fabric and one bib shape from the wadding.
2 Fold the binding fabric in half and trim off the excess to make a square. Cut three 2in (5cm) strips across the grain to make up the bias binding (see Fig 1). Trim off the angled edges and sew the strips together to form a continuous piece.
3 Iron the binding in half lengthways, open it up again and iron the raw edges to the centre ironed line. Set aside.
4 Sandwich the two bib pieces together with the wadding inside, pin and tack (baste) using a long stitch length to secure (see Fig 2).
5 Cut two collar A and B pieces (see Templates) from the binding fabric. Sew the pieces right sides facing, leaving a turning gap in the top edge (see Fig 3). Repeat for the other collar piece.
6 Centre the collar pieces on the top of the bib front and pin in place, then sew the binding around the edge of the bib (see Fig 4). Fold over the opposite side of the binding and hand sew with a whipstitch.
7 To make the ties, fold the remaining bias binding in half to find the centre and pin in place where the collar meets at the centre front of the bib. Sew the ties in position, fold over the opposite side of the binding and whipstitch by hand to secure.
8 Double fold the ends of the binding ties to hide the raw edges and sew. Machine sew the binding ties in half lengthways, as close to the edges as possible.

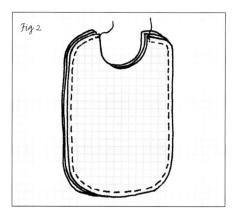

Fig 2

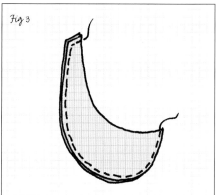

Fig 3

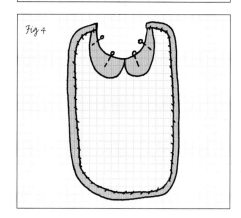

Fig 4

---HANDY TISSUE HOLDERS----

Louise Horler

These little floral holders are the perfect way of storing tissues in your handbag with style. The coordinating flower decoration uses up some of the leftover lining fabric for a pretty finishing touch.

MATERIALS

- ◆ 2 fat quarters of fabric: main and lining
- ◆ Scrap of felt
- ◆ White button

◆ **PATTERN NOTES**
Seam allowance is ⅜in (1cm)

1 Cut out a 6½ × 5½in (16.5 × 14cm) rectangle for the outer layer from main fabric and a 7½ × 5½in (19 × 14cm) rectangle from lining fabric. Place the two fabric rectangles together, pattern sides facing, and sew along each short side; you will have loose fabric on one side.

2 Turn so the pattern side faces out and iron, so a little of the lining fabric is shown at either side of the main fabric. With the main fabric facing you, find the centre point. Fold over both edges to meet here and pin.

3 Sew along the two short sides and trim the edges with pinking shears. Turn right sides out, pushing out the corners with a wooden stick or similar.

4 To make the flower detail, draw around a cotton reel five times on the lining fabric and

cut out the circles. Iron each circle in half and then in half again.

5 Sew running stitch through all the layers, close to the edge along the rounded side of the first quarter circle, then pull tightly to gather. Repeat with each petal, using the same length of thread and ensuring that the petals are close together. When you have finished the fifth petal, knot the end to keep the gathers in place, but do not cut the thread. With the two end petals facing, add a few stitches near the centre of the flower to attach the ends together.

6 Cut a small felt circle for the back and attach the flower with a few small stitches around the inside edge. Sew the button though the fabric of the tissue holder to hold the flower in place.

----HOT WATER BOTTLE COVER----

Lisa Fordham

There's nothing better on a cold winter's day than snuggling up under a blanket with a hot water bottle, and this pretty cover will ensure it stays toasty warm. So simple to make with just two fat quarters, it's the perfect way to beat the winter blues.

MATERIALS

- ◆ 2 fat quarters of fabric: main and lining
- ◆ 10in (25cm) fusible fleece

◆ PATTERN NOTES
Seam allowance is ⅛in (4mm)

1 Using the templates (see Templates) cut the front, back top and back bottom pieces from main fabric, lining fabric and fusible fleece.
2 Starting with the front pieces, place the lining fabric right side down, sandwich the fusible fleece in the centre and place the main fabric right side up on top. Tack (baste) the three layers together around the outer edge.
3 Repeat with the two back sections. This time trim the fusible fleece back 1in (2.5cm) from

the opening on the top and bottom sections before tacking the three sections together.
4 Take the bottom back on the straight edge, fold both fabrics down by ¼in (6mm) and iron. Machine stitch ⅟₁₆in (2mm) from the edge. Repeat with the top back section.
5 Place the front pieces with the main fabric facing up, then the top back with the lining facing up, and then the bottom back sections, also with the lining facing up. Pin to hold, then tack all the way around the three sections. The bottom section should overlap the top section at the opening by approximately 1½in (4cm). Machine stitch around. Remove the tacking, then turn right side out and iron.

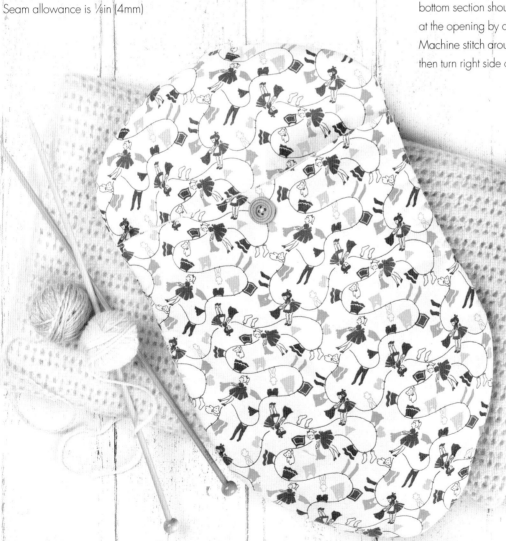

....QUIRKY PENCIL CASE....

Kevin Kosbab

The diagonal zip and bold fabrics make this pencil case truly stand out from the crowd.
Two fat quarters provide enough fabric to make three cases, or simply cut the exterior and
lining from the same fabric and make one case using a single fat quarter.

MATERIALS

- ◆ 2 fat quarters of fabric: main and lining
- ◆ 9in (23cm) zip

◆ PATTERN NOTES

Seam allowance is ¼in (6mm)

1 Using the template provided (see Templates) cut two panels from the right side of the main fabric and two panels from the wrong side of the lining fabric (these will be mirror images of the exterior panels).

2 Cut four 2 x 1in (5 x 2.5cm) zip ends from the main fabric. Fold under ½in (1.2cm) at one short end of each zip end and iron. Pin a zip end to each side, leaving an 8in (20cm) zip length between the creases (see Fig 1).

3 Sew along the creases at one end to join both zip ends to the zip. Repeat at the opposite end and finger press the zip ends

out. Refold the zip ends out of the way then trim ¼in (6mm) beyond each seam. Open the zip ends out again to conceal the raw ends of the zip.

4 Place the zip right sides together with one of the exterior case panels, aligning it with the slanted edge of the panel (see Fig 2).

5 Place a lining case panel wrong side up on top, aligning its edges with the exterior panel and sandwiching the zip between. Pin the layers together along the slanted edge. Using a zip foot, sew along the slanted edge, stopping with the needle down to move the

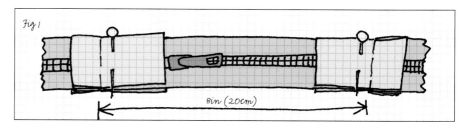

Fig 1

8in (20cm)

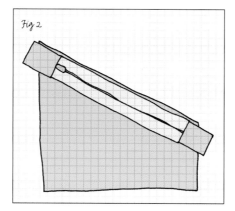

Fig 2

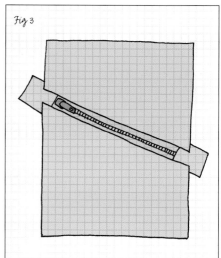

Fig 3

Top Tip

IF YOU ARE USING A PLASTIC ZIP, BE CAREFUL NOT TO MELT THE ZIP TEETH WITH THE IRON!

zip pull behind the needle when necessary. Open out the exterior and lining panels and iron. Repeat to sew the remaining exterior and lining panel to the opposite zip tape. Open all panels out (see Fig 3).

6 Topstitch along each side of the zip through all layers. Trim the zip ends flush with the edges of the exterior and lining panels.

7 Bring the 9in (23cm) edges of the exterior panels right sides together and pin. Sew together, backstitching at both ends and finger press the seam allowances open.

8 Open the zip at least halfway. Bring the long edges of the lining panels right sides together and pin. Sew together, leaving a 4in (10cm) turning gap. Finger press the seam allowances open.

9 Arrange the exterior panels so the seam falls in the centre of the underside; the zip will run diagonally across the top. Sew both short edges together between the zip seam and the bottom corner of the exterior panels. Repeat to sew the short edges of the lining panels.

10 At each end of the zip, sew all layers together between the zip seams. Clip the corners to reduce bulk. Turn right sides out through the opening and gently push the corners out. Fold in the seam allowances along the gap in the lining and sew closed. Stuff the lining into the exterior and iron.

----COLOURFUL CLUTCH PURSE----

Kaye Prince

This striking clutch is the perfect accessory for a night out on the town. The eye-catching handle accents the purse beautifully; and with interior card pockets and a sturdy zip, you can be sure all your treasures will be safely stored.

MATERIALS

- 2 fat quarters of fabric in contrasting colours
- 1 fat quarter of medium weight interfacing
- Scrap of leather
- 12in (30cm) zip

♦ PATTERN NOTES
Seam allowance is ½in (1.3cm), unless stated otherwise

1 From the first fat quarter cut the following: two 10 × 12in (25 × 30cm) rectangles for the purse, two 3½ × 4¼in (9 × 11cm) and one 6½ × 4¼in (16.5 × 11cm) rectangles for the interior card pockets.

2 From the second fat quarter cut the following: two 10 × 12in (25 × 30cm) rectangles for the lining, two 10 × 3in (25 × 7.5cm) rectangles for the strap and two 1¼ × 2¼in (3.5 × 5.5cm) rectangles for the zip tabs. Now cut one 10 × 3in (25 × 7.5cm) and two 10 × 12in (25 × 30cm) rectangles from the interfacing.

3 To make the strap, first fuse the smaller rectangle of interfacing to one fabric strap piece. With right sides facing, sew two strap pieces together on each long side. Turn right side out, iron and topstitch along each long edge.

4 Fuse the larger interfacing pieces to each purse outer piece. Measure approximately 4½in (11.5cm) up from the bottom of one purse outer piece, lay the assembled handle across, matching the raw edges, and tack (baste) in place along the short sides.

5 To make the interior card pockets fold each rectangle in half widthways, right sides facing, and iron. Sew along the three open sides on each, using a ¼in (6mm) seam allowance and leaving an opening in the long side for turning. Turn each piece and iron.

6 Topstitch each of the smaller pieces along the long folded edge. Measure 1in (2.5cm) from the bottom of the larger piece and lay a smaller piece across. Sew in place along the bottom edge and sides using a very narrow topstitch. Lay the second smaller piece flush with the bottom edge of the larger piece and stitch in place. Measure 3½in (9cm) up from the bottom of one lining piece and centre the completed pocket piece, then stitch in place.

7 Evenly trim the zip to 9½in (24cm). Iron each short edge of a tab piece ¼in (6mm) in towards the wrong side, then fold in half widthways. Repeat for the other tab. Fit the zip end inside the tab, butting it against the fold, and topstitch in place across the ironed down edge. Repeat at the other end.

8 Line up the long edge of the zip itself (not the tab). Centre and place it, zip side down, along the top edge of one outer panel, right side up. Place one lining panel, right side down, on top and pin. Stitch through all three layers using your zipper foot.

9 Turn the panel right sides out so the lining and outer pieces are wrong sides together and iron. Place the second outer piece right side up on a surface and lay the piece just sewn on top, zip side down. Centre and line up the zip edge along the top edge of this second panel. Place the lining right side down on top. Stitch through all three layers using the zipper foot.

10 Turn the panel right side out so the lining and outer pieces are wrong sides together and iron. Topstitch the fabric together along each zip edge.

11 Cut a small rectangle of leather and fold in half widthways. Iron and align the raw edges along one side of an outer piece, about 1 in (2.5cm) from the zip and tack in place.

12 Open the zip at least three-quarters of the way. Fold the purse so both the lining and outer pieces are aligned right sides together and stitch all the way around, leaving a turning gap in the bottom of the lining. Turn through to right sides, using a wooden stick or similar to push out the corners. Stitch the gaps closed and iron.

Top Tip

TO ENSURE YOUR ZIP HAS NEAT CORNERS, FOLD THE TABS TOWARDS THE OUTER PIECES AND THE SEAMS TOWARDS THE LINING PIECES.

----TIME FOR TEA COSY----

Liz Betts

This tea cosy is durable enough for everyday use, but also looks lovely just displayed on a dresser. Use two layers of wadding (batting) to keep the teapot extra warm. The design is perfect for off-cuts so, if you are a quilter, have a rummage through your scrap wadding box.

MATERIALS

- 3 fat quarters of fabric
- Four 13 × 17½in (33 × 44.5cm) pieces of cotton wadding (batting)
- Two 13 × 17½in (33 × 44.5cm) pieces of calico

◆ PATTERN NOTES

Seam allowance is ¼in (6mm)

Top Tip

THE TEMPLATE FITS A LARGE TEAPOT, BUT CAN EASILY BE ADJUSTED TO FIT A SMALLER POT.

1 Draw around the tea cosy template (see Templates) onto a piece of card and cut out.
2 Cut the first fat quarter lengthways to make four 3 × 22in (7.5 × 55cm) strips, then cut these into 38 rectangles measuring 2 × 3in (5 × 7.5cm). From the remaining piece, cut a 15½ × 5in (39.5 × 13cm) section for the lining. Cut eight 1¾ × 2in (4.5 × 5cm) rectangles from the leftover pieces.
3 Repeat Step 2 with the second fat quarter; this time cutting the four 3 × 22in (7.5 × 55cm) strips into 40 rectangles measuring 2 × 3in (5 × 7.5cm).
4 Lay the fabric rectangles out to make two panels, each seven rectangles high and six across. Alternate between the different fabrics, as shown (see Fig 1). Stitch each panel together, sewing the rows together first and then ironing the seams.

5 Place a calico piece on top of the two wadding pieces. Centre an ironed patchwork panel on top, holding the layers together with quilter's safety pins. Repeat with the other panel. Machine quilt straight horizontal lines across the centre of each row. Draw around the template on top of the patchwork and cut, then repeat for the other side.

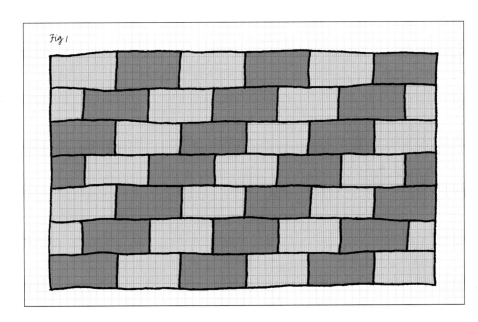

Fig 1

Top Tip

USE A WALKING FOOT FOR MACHINE QUILTING (IF YOU HAVE ONE) AND A SLIGHTLY LONGER STITCH LENGTH THAN YOU WOULD FOR PIECING.

6 Cut the following from the third fat quarter: two 2¼ × 22in (5.5 × 55cm) strips for the binding, two 15½ × 6½in (39.5 × 16.5cm) strips for the lining, and two 2½ × 4in (6 × 10cm) handle pieces.

7 Stitch down the two long edges of each handle, right sides facing. Turn inside out, iron and topstitch ¼in (6mm) from the edge along the long sides. Fold in half so the raw ends are together.

8 Lay the panels on top of each other, right sides facing. Centre the handle at the curved top edge, with raw edges aligned. Pin and stitch around the sides and curved top and turn out.

9 For the lining, take the two 15½ × 5in (39.5 × 13cm) sections cut in Step 2 and the two 15½ × 6½in (39.5 × 16.5cm) strips cut in Step 6. Sew together a 5in (13cm) and a 6½in (16.5cm) wide strip along the length to make a 15½ × 11½in (39.5 × 29cm) strip. Repeat for the other two pieces and iron.

10 Draw around the tea cosy template on the wrong side of one of the fabric pieces and cut. Repeat for the other fabric piece. With right sides facing, sew the sides and curved top of the two pieces. Tuck the lining inside the tea cosy, wrong sides facing, and pin around the raw edge at the bottom.

11 For the binding, stitch the two 2¼ × 22in (5.5 × 55cm) strips together. Iron the join, fold in half widthways, wrong sides together, then iron again. Fold ¼in (6mm) of fabric to the wrong side of one end to create the hem.

12 Place the raw edge of the binding strip level with the raw edge of the tea cosy. Pin and start sewing, leaving a 1½in (4cm) tail of binding (the folded end), and sew around the bottom. Sew around the sides, open the seams to divide the bulk of the wadding and stop sewing 2½in (6cm) before the end. Tuck the binding raw edge inside the folded edge and cut the excess. Pin and stitch over the join.

13 Fold the binding inside the tea cosy, and slipstitch through the lining and wadding, without sewing through to the front.

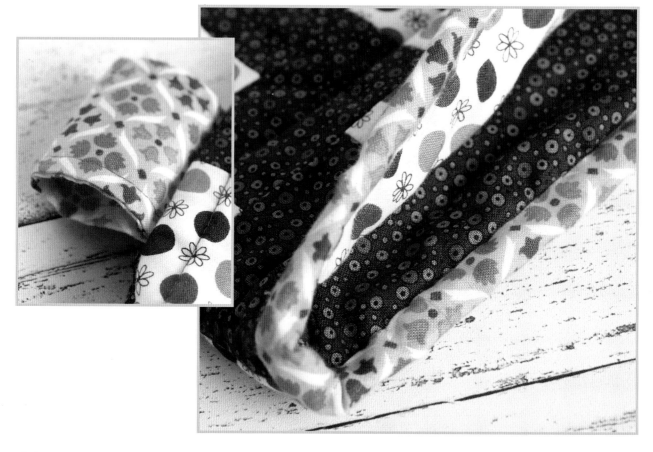

----QUILTED OVEN MITT----

Jessie Fincham

This practical oven mitt will make an attractive addition to your kitchen accessories. The coordinating binding, hanging loop and crosshatch quilting detail give this cooking essential a professional finishing touch.

MATERIALS

- 3 fat quarters of fabric: inner, outer and binding
- 20in (50cm) wadding (batting)

1 Sandwich the wadding (batting) between the inner and outer fabric and pin to secure.

2 Using the template provided (see Templates), draw a mitt shape onto the sandwiched layers of fabric, then turn the template over and draw an opposite mitt shape. Cut a rough rectangle around each mitt, leaving 1in (2.5cm) around the edge.

3 Quilt straight lines with a 1in (2.5cm) spacing to create a crosshatch effect (see Fig 1). Repeat for the other mitt, then cut out the mitt shapes.

4 Fold the binding fabric in half and trim off the excess to make a square. Cut one 2in (5cm) strip across the diagonal to create bias binding. Iron the binding in half lengthways, open up again and iron the raw edges to the centre ironed line.

5 Sew the binding to the bottom outside edge of the mitt, leaving a few inches for a 'tail' at the start. Once you reach the finished point, iron the binding strips and mark a pencil line. Sew along this line and trim off the excess. Fold over the opposite side of the binding and hand or machine sew.

6 Make a hanging loop by trimming off an 8in (20cm) length of binding. Fold in half lengthways and sew very close to the edge. Fold in half to create a loop and pin to the outer side of the mitt.

7 Place both mitt pieces right sides together and sew around the edge with a ¼in (6mm) seam allowance, using a walking foot to feed through the thick layers. Sew the hanging loop in place at the same time. Zigzag stitch around the edge and trim off any excess. Turn the mitt right sides out, pushing out the edges with a wooden stick or similar.

Top Tip

WHEN DRAWING AROUND THE TEMPLATES, MAKE SURE YOU LEAVE ENOUGH SPACE BETWEEN EACH SHAPE AND THE EDGES OF THE FABRIC.

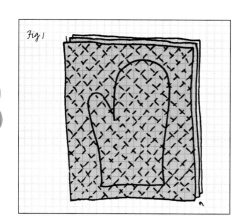

Fig 1

----BABY BEAR'S QUILT----

Cynthia Shaffer

Children will adore playing with this cute little quilt made from just three fat quarters; the perfect size for a much-loved teddy bear's bed or a doll's picnic blanket. Alternate panels and strips of your favourite coordinating fabrics to create the quilt pattern.

MATERIALS

- 3 fat quarters of fabric: blue teacup design, pink and white toile, blue and light green toile
- 16 × 18in (40.5 × 46cm) white flannel
- 7 white buttons
- 30in (75cm) each of double wide binding in pink and bright yellow

◆ PATTERN NOTES

Seam allowance is ¼in (6mm)

1 Fussy cut four 14½ × 2¾in (37 × 7cm) strips from the blue teacup design fat quarter.

2 Cut eight 3¼ × 3in (8 × 7.5cm) rectangles from pink toile and seven rectangles of the same size from blue toile.

3 Alternate the pink and blue toile panels to make a row of five panels, starting and ending with pink. Repeat to make a second row. Repeat again, this time starting and ending with blue.

4 Stitch the teacup design fabric strips cut in Step 1 to the alternating pieced panel strips, as shown in the photograph. Iron the pieced panel.

5 Cut a 16 × 18in (40.5 × 46cm) panel from blue and light green toile. Place face down then layer with the flannel panel and the pieced panel. Pin all three layers together.

6 Cut the pink and bright yellow binding into two 15in (38cm) lengths. Iron the binding in half, pin over the seams, and stitch in place. Machine quilt in the ditch of the seams where the binding has not been stitched.

7 Cut 1¾ × 70in (4.5 × 178cm) strips from pink toile – you will need to cut and stitch several segments of fabric together to give you 70in (178cm) widths. Bind the outer edge of the quilt.

8 Stitch a white button into the centre of each blue toile panel.

----HOOKED ON YOU ROLL----

Ali Burdon

This gorgeous roll opens up to display a variety of divider pockets, perfect for crochet hooks, scissors and all your sewing sundries. The pockets can be customized to any desired width to fit all your items and the pretty ties will ensure they are all kept safe.

MATERIALS

- 3 fat quarters of fabric: coordinating main, contrast and lining
- 10in (25cm) low loft fusible fleece
- 10in (25cm) medium weight interfacing

1 Cut the following from the main fabric: one 9¾ × 13in (24.5 × 33cm) piece for the outer – the 13in (33cm) measurement should be parallel with the selvedge if your fabric is directional; one 5 × 15in (13 × 38cm) piece for the pocket and two 2 × 4in (5 × 10cm) pieces for the tie tabs.

2 Cut the following from the contrast fabric: one 2½ × 13in (6.5 × 33cm) piece, one 4¼ × 13in (11 × 33cm) piece for the outer contrast sections and one 2 × 15in (5 × 38cm) piece for the pocket binding.

3 Cut the following from the lining fabric: one 13 × 15in (33 × 38cm) piece for the main lining, one 5 × 15in (13 × 38cm) piece for the pocket lining and two 1¾ × 18in (4.5 × 46cm) pieces for the ties.

4 Cut one 13 × 15in (33 × 38cm) piece from the fusible fleece and one 13 × 15in (33 × 38cm) piece from the interfacing.

5 Fold one of the tie pieces in half lengthways, finger pressing to crease. Unfold, fold the two edges into the crease and iron them into place. Fold in half down the central crease and iron again, then stitch the long open edge closed. Topstitch the folded edge to match and repeat.

6 Fold a tie tab piece in half lengthways and fold the two edges into the middle crease, as before. Keep the edges folded in and fold in half widthways this time. Unfold and iron the two short edges into this crease. Fold down the middle again to create a square with the raw edges hidden, then iron. Unfold the last fold, then fold the tab around the end of one of the completed ties, with the end next to the short crease in the tie tab. Pin or glue into place then stitch around the tab close to the edge. Repeat.

7 Pin the 4¼ × 13in (11 × 33cm) piece of contrast fabric right sides facing with the left hand edge of the 9¾ × 13in (24.5 × 33cm) main fabric piece. Pin, stitch with a ¼in (6mm) seam, then iron the seam towards the main fabric.

8 Place the partially completed outer section right side up, with the contrast section on the left. On the right-hand edge of the main fabric, measure 4½in (11.5cm) from the

bottom corner and mark this point on the right side. Pin the completed ties – one on top of the other – at this point, with the raw edges slightly overlapping the right-hand edge of the fabric. Lay the 2½ x 13in (6.5 x 33cm) contrast fabric right sides facing with the right-hand edge of the main fabric, so the ties are sandwiched inbetween. Pin, then stitch with a ¼in (6mm) seam. Iron this seam sideways towards the main fabric.

9 Fuse the fusible fleece to the wrong side of the outer section, following the manufacturer's instructions. Topstitch the main fabric of the outer section, close to the two seam lines, with the contrast fabric. Strengthen the area where the ties are placed, stitching a rectangle and cross across the seam line and the tie ends.

10 Iron the interfacing on the large piece of lining fabric, following the manufacturer's instructions. Iron a 5 x 15in (13 x 38cm) piece of interfacing to the outer pocket piece.

11 Iron the 2 x 15in (5 x 38cm) piece of binding fabric in half lengthways to crease. Fold the edges in towards the centre and iron again.

12 Put the two pocket pieces wrong sides together and pin one of the unfolded raw edges of the binding, right sides together, on the front top edge of the pocket. Pin in place, then stitch along the first fold line on the binding – about ½in (1.2cm) from the top edge of the pocket. Fold the binding up and round to the back of the pocket and slipstitch in place on the back. Topstitch the binding at the bottom edge.

13 Position the lining side of the completed pocket against the right side of the main inner fabric, aligning the bottom edges. Pin in place, then zigzag stitch or tack (baste) along the two short sides of the pocket and the bottom edge.

14 To ensure the wrap folds neatly, stitch fold lines on the pocket. Measure 4½in (11.5cm) from the right-hand edge and mark and stitch a division line, then make another line of stitching ¼in (6mm) to the left. Repeat, making a line on the pocket 4½in (11.5cm) from the left-hand edge, and another line ¼in (6mm) to the right of it. Reverse stitch at both ends of your sewing. At the top of the pocket, pull the top thread through to the back and knot with the bobbin thread.

15 You can stitch a number of pockets of your desired width between the two fold areas. I stitched a mixture of divisions between ¾in (2cm) and 2in (5cm) wide, including one wider 2½in (6.5cm) pocket for a pair of scissors. Leave ½in (1.2cm) clear at either edge for the side seams, reverse stitching as in Step 14.

16 Pin the inner and outer sections right sides together and stitch the bottom and sides with a ½in (1.2cm) seam, leaving the top edge. Tuck the ties out of the way into one of the pockets.

17 Mark the seam line ½in (1.2cm) from the top edge. Use a curved edge with a 3–3½in (7.5–9cm) diameter to mark curved corners for the top edge, joining the line of the stitched side seams with the line of the marked top seam. Stitch the top edge, leaving a 3–4in (7.5–10cm) turning gap. Trim the seams to ¼in (6mm).

18 Turn right side out and push out the corners with a wooden stick or similar. Iron the wrap, turning under the raw edges of the opening. Stitch the gap closed either using ladder stitch or by temporarily gluing or pinning the edges in place. Topstitch around the entire wrap, then fasten off.

TRADITIONAL CHRISTMAS STOCKING

Louise Horler

Guaranteed to delight children – or the young at heart – on Christmas morning; this gorgeous stocking is simple to stitch from just three fat quarters. Make it extra special by sewing the recipient's name onto the cuff.

MATERIALS

- Three fat quarters of fabric: main, lining and contrasting pattern for cuff
- 9in (23cm) ribbon
- Decorative button

◆ PATTERN NOTES

Seam allowance is ⅜in (1cm)

1 Fold the main fat quarter in half. Pin the template (see Templates) on top and cut two stocking shapes. Repeat with the lining fabric.
2 Fold the contrasting fat quarter in half and cut two stocking cuff pieces (see Templates). Place the long edge of the stocking cuff face down on top of one of the main stocking pieces and sew along the top. Fold out flat. Repeat with the other side of the cuff, this time sewing onto a lining stocking. You will now have a main stocking, cuff and lining stocking sewn together, each with the pattern sides facing up. Make sure that the feet face the same way. Iron each seam towards the cuff. Repeat with the remaining fabric pieces to make two long stocking shapes.
3 Place one stocking piece on a work surface and the other face down on top, ensuring that the main and lining fabrics are matched, then pin around. Starting halfway across the base

of the lining foot, machine stitch around the foot, up one side of the leg, around the other side of the leg, and down to the bottom of the lining foot, leaving a small turning gap in the bottom of the lining foot. Trim around the fabric with pinking shears to prevent fraying and reduce bulk.
4 Pull the main stocking fabric through the gap in the lining foot, turn inside out so the fabric patterns show, and iron. Neatly iron under the fabric at the gap in the lining fabric and machine stitch closed.
5 Push the stocking lining back inside the main stocking until the lining 'foot' is neatly inside the main stocking and iron again. Fold over the stocking cuff.
6 Attach a ribbon hanging loop and a button for decoration inside the stocking top. The stitching can be hidden on the back by the stocking cuff.

----ELEGANT E-READER CASE----

Kaye Prince

This simple-to-sew case is designed to fit a 7in (18cm) tablet or e-reader. As well as looking chic, it is handy for protecting your tablets from scratches and knocks while you're on the go.

MATERIALS

- 3 fat quarters of fabric
- 1 fat quarter of medium weight interfacing
- 1 fat quarter of quilt wadding (batting)
- ¾in (2cm) button

◆ PATTERN NOTES
Seam allowance is ½in (1.2cm)

1 From the first fat quarter cut two 6½ × 9½in (16.5 × 24cm) rectangles for the outer panels and two 6 × 4½in (15 × 11.5cm) rectangles for the flap.

2 From the second fat quarter cut one 6½ × 7½in (16.5 × 19cm) rectangle for the outer pocket.

3 From the third fat quarter cut two 6½ × 9½in (16.5 × 24cm) rectangles for lining, one 6½ × 7½in (16.5 × 19cm) rectangle for pocket lining, and one 1¼ × 4in (3 × 10cm) rectangle for the button loop.

4 From medium weight interfacing cut a 6½ × 7½in (16.5 × 19cm) and a 6 × 4½in (15 × 11.5cm) rectangle. Cut two 6½ × 9½in (16.5 × 24cm) rectangles from quilt wadding.

5 Layer one outer panel with one quilt wadding panel, pin together and tack (baste). Quilt with vertical lines ½in (1.2cm) apart. Trim the quilted panel down to 6½ × 9½in (16.5 × 24cm) if necessary. Repeat with the other outer and wadding panels.

6 Fuse the 6½ × 7½in (16.5 × 19cm) piece of interfacing to the outer pocket rectangle. Place the outer pocket and pocket lining pieces right sides together and sew along one short side. Turn right side out so the wrong sides are together, iron and topstitch along the seamed edge. Sew the button to the pocket, 2in (5cm) from topstitched edge.

7 Fold the button loop piece in half lengthways with right sides together and sew along one long edge. Turn right side out, iron, and topstitch along the two long sides. Fuse the second interfacing piece to one flap rectangle. Loop the button loop piece and with the raw edges aligned tack to the flap piece. Place both flap pieces right sides together and stitch around one long and two short sides. Turn right sides out, iron, and topstitch along the three seamed edges.

8 Line up the pocket piece, wrong sides together, on top of one outer panel and tack in place. Place the outer pieces wrong sides together and sew along the bottom and sides. Turn right side out and iron. With the raw edges aligned, match the flap piece along the back top edge of the case and tack in place.

9 Place the lining pieces wrong sides together and sew along the bottom and sides, leaving a turning gap in the bottom. Place the outer pouch inside the lining, so the right sides touch, and stitch around the top edge. Turn right side out using the turning gap, then iron and sew the gap in the lining closed. Finally, topstitch along the pouch opening.

Top Tip

YOU CAN MAKE A SMALLER VERSION OF THE E-READER CASE TO FIT YOUR SMART PHONE.

----TEA PARTY PILLOWCASE DRESS----

Prudence Rogers

This cute dress is ideal for girls of six months to two years. The simplicity of the design means it is forgiving when it comes to sizing, as only the length and armholes need to be adjusted for age. When it becomes too short to wear as a dress, it will make a lovely top!

MATERIALS

- 3 fat quarters of fabric
- 40in (1m) cream lace
- 40in (1m) linen ribbon, ½in (1.5cm) wide
- 12in (30cm) pale pink ready-made bias binding

1 Pre-wash and iron the fat quarters. Cut four 8¼in (21cm) wide rectangles: two from the first fabric and two from the second. To determine the length, measure from the bottom of the neck to where you'd like the hem to finish and take off 1in (2.5cm) to allow for the border with seam allowances to be added.

2 With one rectangle of each fabric right sides together, pin and sew with a ¼in (6mm) seam allowance along the long side. Zigzag stitch together the two raw edges to finish the seam and iron the allowance to one side. Repeat with the other two rectangles.

3 Cut two 15¾ × 4¼in (40 × 11cm) rectangles from the third fat quarter. With right sides together, pin the long edge to the bottom (short) edge of one dress panel and sew with a ¼in (6mm) seam allowance. Neaten the edges with zigzag stitch and iron to one side, as before. If your fabric is directional, ensure your panel is the right way up before adding the border along the bottom edge (see Fig 1). Repeat with the other rectangle and dress panel.

4 Lay the two dress pieces right sides together and pin. Fold the dress in half lengthways, lining up the edges. To make the armholes, measure down from the top – 4¾in (12cm) for smaller sizes or 5½in (14cm) for larger sizes – and 2¼in (5.5cm) in from the raw edge side, and join together in a 'J' shape. Cut through all four layers to create armholes on both sides (see Fig 2). Open out the dress.

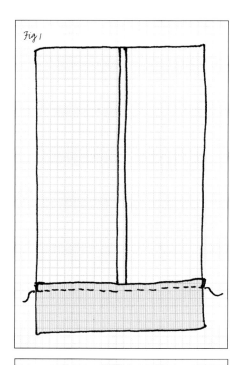

Fig 1

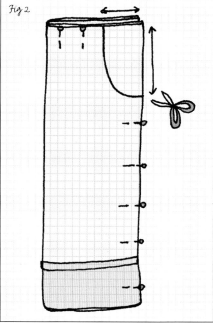

Fig 2

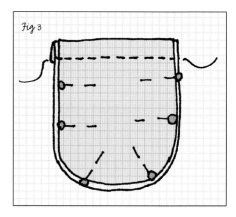

Fig 3

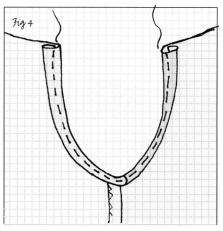

Fig 4

5 Cut a pocket from the border fabric using the template (see Templates). Cut out the inner part from card, place it in the centre of the pocket on the wrong side, and iron a ¼in (6mm) seam allowance around the sides and curved bottom. Remove the card template.

6 Fold the bias binding in half lengthways; pin it around the sides and bottom of the back of the pocket with ⅛in (2–3mm) protruding from the edge. Fold over and iron the top edge of the pocket under by ½in (1.2cm); topstitch across the top of the pocket with a ¼in (6mm) seam allowance (see Fig 3).

7 Pin the pocket to the centre of the front dress panel, 1½in (4cm) from the border fabric, allowing ¼in (6mm) on the raw edge for the seam allowance. Topstitch close to the fold, leaving the top open and making triangles in the top corners to add strength.

8 Place the two dress panels right sides together. Sew up to the armhole on each side with a ¼in (6mm) seam allowance. Finish the seam with zigzag stitch and iron to one side.

9 Keeping right sides together, open out the dress in the other direction so the armholes are flat and line up. Fold over and iron a ¼in (6mm) fold around the armhole, then fold again by ¼in (6mm) to hide the raw edge. Pin into place. Repeat for the other armhole, then neatly topstitch around the armholes, close to the folded edge.

10 Lay the dress flat with right sides still together, fold down the neckline by ¼in (6mm) and iron. Fold down a further ¾in (2cm) and iron, concealing the raw edge. Pin into place to create the casing for the ribbon. Turn the dress over and repeat on the other side, making sure the top edges line up. Sew close to the bottom edge of the fold, creating a space through which the ribbon can be threaded (see Fig 4).

11 With right sides together, fold the bottom edge of the dress by ¼in (6mm) all the way around. Iron into place, then fold up a further ½in (1.2cm) to make the hem. Iron flat, concealing the raw edge and pin.

12 Measure around the hem and cut a piece of lace 1in (2.5cm) longer than

this measurement. Pin the lace around the hem, keeping it flat against the fabric and overlapping the folded hem by about ⅜in (1cm). Overlap the two lace ends and pin, right sides together. Stitch the ends together, pulling away slightly from the dress fabric (sew the lace only at this stage), then trim the seam to ¼in (6mm). Pin the joined ends back to the hem, then sew ¼in (6mm) from the edge around the hem, topstitching the concealed hem and attaching the lace at the same time.

13 Turn the dress out to right sides and iron. Cut two lengths of ribbon, each three times the length of the dress neck width. With a safety pin attached to one end, thread a ribbon through each casing, making sure they lie flat. Heat-seal the ends of the ribbons to prevent fraying by holding them next to (not in) a flame.

14 Using the centre seam to hide the stitching, sew a vertical line across the casing to hold the ribbon in place. Repeat for the other ribbon to finish.

Top Tip

REVERSE STITCH A FEW TIMES AT EACH END OF THE CASING TO ENSURE THAT THE EDGES ARE STRONG AND THE THREADS DON'T COME UNDONE.

----STYLISH SATCHEL----

Emily Levey

The trend-setting tween will adore this sweet little satchel bag featuring a cross-body strap, a contrasting front pocket and a flap closure to keep valuables safe! Make it in her favourite fabrics to flatter her current style.

MATERIALS

- 3 fat quarters of fabric: main, lining and pocket
- 20in (50cm) cotton quilter's wadding (batting)
- Two 2in (5cm) squares of firm iron-on interfacing
- Magnetic popper (snap) fastener

◆ PATTERN NOTES
Seam allowance is ⅝in (1.5cm)

1 From the main fabric, lining fabric and wadding, cut two 10in (25cm) squares for the main body of the bag and an 8 × 4½in (20 × 11.5cm) rectangle for the flap.

2 Trace around a plate or another rounded object at both bottom corners of the flap fabric and trim the corners away. Repeat on the flap lining and wadding.

3 Cut a 7in (18cm) square from the pocket fabric, lining fabric and wadding. From the pocket fabric cut a 6 × 22in (15 × 55cm) and a 6 × 8in (15 × 20cm) rectangle for the handle. Now cut a 1⅜ × 28½in (3.5 × 72cm) rectangle from wadding. If your wadding is not large enough to cut this in one piece, join scraps together using zigzag stitch.

4 Take the lining fabric flap piece and make a central mark 1⅜in (3.5cm) from the bottom edge on the wrong side. Position the small square of interfacing over this mark and fuse with an iron. Following the manufacturer's instructions, insert one side of the magnetic fastener over this mark.

5 Lay the two flap fabric pieces right sides together and place the wadding on top of the main fabric. You can use basting spray to tack (baste) the wadding to the fabric piece. Pin around the bottom curved edge and sew along. Trim the seam allowance to reduce bulk, turn the right way out and iron well. Topstitch ¼in (6mm) from the edge along the curved edge. Tack the top opening closed and set aside.

6 Sew the strap fabric pieces together along the short edge and iron the seam open to make a 6 × 28½in (15 × 72cm) strap. Iron in half with wrong sides together along the

length and open out. Bring the two outer edges into the centre and iron again. Tuck the long wadding strip under one of these folds and fold the strap in half again. You should have a long strap about 1½in (4cm) wide with all the raw edges enclosed. Pin along the length, topstitch ⅛in (2.5mm) from the edge down both long sides (see Fig 1) and set aside.

7 Repeat Step 4 with the main fabric pocket piece and the remaining side of the magnetic fastener, this time making a central mark 1⅜in (3.5cm) down from the top edge on the wrong side of the flap.

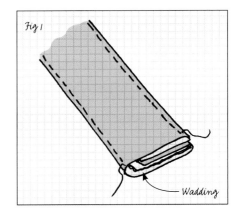

Fig 1

Wadding

8 Lay the two pocket fabric pieces right sides together and place the wadding on top of the lining fabric (it is useful to use basting spray here). Pin around all four sides and sew around, leaving a 3¼in (8cm) opening in the bottom edge. Sew slowly past the magnetic fastener, making sure you keep straight. A walking foot can be used to stitch through all the layers.

9 Trim the corners of the pocket piece and turn the right way out. Iron well, taking care to tuck in the unsewn edges of the opening and line up neatly. Pin the pocket centrally on the front of one of the 10in (25cm) main bag fabric square pieces, 1⅜in (3.5cm) down from the top edge. Topstitch ⅛in (2.5mm) from the edge along the two sides and bottom edge, leaving the top edge open (see Fig 2).

10 Take the two 10in (25cm) square lining pieces and pin together with right sides facing along the two sides and bottom edge, leaving the top edge open. Stitch around these three sides, leaving a 4in (10cm) turning gap in the centre of the bottom edge. Trim the corners, turn through to the right sides and set aside.

11 Tack the two 10cm (25cm) square wadding pieces onto the wrong sides of the two 10cm (25cm) square main fabric pieces using basting spray. Place the completed flap section centrally onto the top edge of the bag back piece (without the pocket), with the lining facing up and the main prints facing each other. Tack in place, stitching ⅜in (1cm) from the edge.

12 Place the two outer bag pieces with right sides facing and pin along the sides and bottom edge, leaving the top edge open. Stitch around the three edges and trim the corners.

13 Tack (baste) the completed handle in place on the outer bag section. Line up the handle centrally over the side seams of the bag, with the short raw edge in line with the top edge of the bag and the bulk down inside the bag (see Fig 3).

14 Put the lining inside the outer bag section, with right sides together. Pin then stitch around the top edge. Turn the bag right sides out through the turning gap in the lining. Iron well and slipstitch the opening closed.

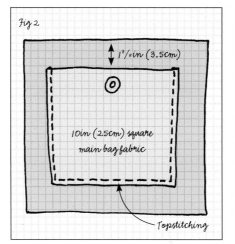

Fig 2

1⅜in (3.5cm)

10in (25cm) square main bag fabric

Topstitching

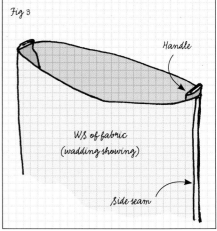

Fig 3

Handle

W/S of fabric (wadding showing)

Side seam

FARMYARD SEWING MACHINE COVER

Cynthia Shaffer

I love the fun theme of this farmyard print fabric, which is beautifully complemented by the bold green tree and pocket appliqué details. What better way to protect your sewing machine, while keeping it looking fresh and vibrant at your workstation?

MATERIALS

- 3 fat quarters of print fabric: 2 brown, 1 green
- 9in (23cm) square of fusible web

1 Using the brown print fabric, cut two 7 × 5½in (18 × 14cm) panels. With right sides facing, stitch the panels together with a ½in (1.2cm) seam allowance, matching the long edges. Iron the seam open.

2 Using the template (see Templates), trace the tree onto the paper side of the fusible web. Cut out approximately ½in (1.2cm) from the traced edge. Place the web side down onto the wrong side of the green print fabric and fuse, following the manufacturer's instructions. Cut out the tree and peel off the paper backing. Place the green tree on the brown stitched fabric, 3in (7.5cm) from the bottom and left side and fuse in place.

3 Stitch around the tree in off-white perle cotton using long running stitches and an occasional overcast stitch.

4 Cut a 5¼in (13.5cm) square pocket from the green print fabric. Iron the top edge under by 1in (2.5cm) then stitch in place.

5 Trace the pocket panel (see Templates) onto the paper side of the fusible web, cut out and fuse to the brown fabric, as in Step 2. Centre the brown pocket panel 1½in (4cm) from the bottom of the pocket and fuse, as before. Repeat Step 3 to stitch around the panel.

6 Iron the sides and the bottom edge of the pocket under by ½in (1.2cm). Pin to the sewing machine cover, 3½in (9cm) up from the bottom and right side, and stitch in place.

7 Cut five 1½ × 20in (4 × 50cm) strips from green fabric. Stitch the short ends together to make a 1½ × 100in (4 × 250cm) strip. Iron in half widthways then iron the edges into the ironed fold to create a binding strip.

8 Stitch the binding around the outer edge of the cover. Now sew running stitches around the binding using off-white perle cotton.

9 Cut four 2 × 13in (5 × 32cm) green fabric strips. Iron in half widthways, iron the edges into the fold and stitch the strip together. Stitch these strips to the inside of all four sides of the cover, 5½in (14cm) from the bottom edges.

----CHEF'S POTHOLDER----

Jessie Fincham

This pretty potholder is an essential in the kitchen and is so simple to sew using the template provided. It perfectly complements the Quilted Oven Mitt to make a lovely gift set for somebody that likes to cook.

MATERIALS

- ◆ 3 fat quarters of fabric: 2 main, 1 binding
- ◆ 50cm (20in) wadding (batting)

1 Sandwich the wadding between the two main fat quarters. Secure with pins.

2 Using the template (see Templates), draw two potholder shapes onto the fabric, leaving enough space between each edge and the edges of the fabric. Cut out a rough square around each design, leaving about 1in (2.5cm) around the edge.

3 Quilt straight lines with a 1in (2.5cm) spacing to create a crosshatch effect. Cut out the potholder shape.

4 Repeat Steps 1–3 using the pocket template (see Templates) to make the pocket section.

5 Fold the binding fabric in half and trim off the excess to make a square. Cut three 2in (5cm) strips across the diagonal to create the bias binding. Trim off the angled edges and sew the strips together to form one long, continuous piece.

6 Iron the binding in half lengthways, open up again and iron the raw edges into the centre ironed line. Machine sew the binding to the straight edge of the pocket.

7 Cut an 8in (20cm) length strip from the binding for the hanging loop. Fold lengthways and sew very close to the edge. Fold to create a loop and pin to the potholder, with the loop facing inwards.

8 Place the pocket on top of the main section and sew very close to the edges (see Fig 1).

9 Sew the binding all around the potholder, leaving a few inches for a tail at the start and sewing the hanging loop into position as you stitch. Once you reach the finished point, iron the binding strips and mark a pencil line. Sew on this pencil line and trim the excess. Fold over the opposite side of the binding and hand or machine sew to secure.

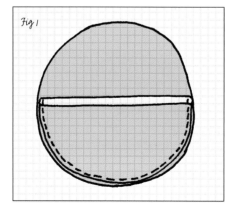

----CLASSIC ROUND BASKET----

Ali Burdon

This versatile vintage-style basket made from three fat quarters is so useful for extra storage in the kitchen. Use it to hold small packets or eggs, or fill it with fruit as a pretty fabric alternative to a fruit bowl.

MATERIALS

- 3 fat quarters of fabric: main, lining and edging
- 10in (25cm) flexi-firm fusible interfacing
- 10in (25cm) medium loft fusible fleece
- 10in (25cm) medium weight fusible interfacing

◆ PATTERN NOTES

Seam allowance is ¼in (6mm)

1 Cut a 9in (23cm) diameter circle and two 3 × 14in (7.5 × 35cm) rectangles from the main fabric and lining fabric. Cut four 2 × 14in (5 × 35cm) rectangles from the edging fabric.

2 Cut a 9in (23cm) diameter circle and a 4½ × 27½in (11.5 × 70cm) rectangle from flexi-firm fusible interfacing, medium loft fusible fleece and medium weight fusible interfacing.

3 Take one of the 3 × 14in (7.5 × 35cm) main fabric pieces and pin one of the edging pieces to the top edge, right sides together. Stitch then iron the seam open. Repeat for the other main fabric and lining pieces.

4 To add a decorative fabric tab to the side of your basket (optional), cut a 3 × 2½in (7.5 × 6.5cm) piece from your desired fabric. Make a crease down the centre, parallel with the 2.5in (6.5cm) edges, fold the edges into the middle crease, then fold along the crease.

Iron then stitch closed, near to the edge, and then topstitch the folded edge to match. Fold in half again to create the tab. Pin the folded tab to one of the outer sections, right sides together, with the raw edges of the tab aligned with one of the short sides. Position about 1¾in (4.5cm) from the top edge.

5 Pin the two outer sections, right sides together, and stitch down one short edge (sandwiching the tab). Iron the seam open and the tab endings to one side. Repeat for the two lining pieces.

6 Fuse the flexi-firm interfacing to the wrong side of the outer section, then fuse the fusible fleece on top of the interfacing, following the manufacturer's instructions. Fuse the circular piece of flexi-firm interfacing to the main fabric circle, then fuse the fusible fleece on top.

Top Tip

YOU MAY NEED TO STRETCH THE BASE SECTION A LITTLE TO GET IT TO FIT. USE LOTS OF PINS (AT LEAST ONE EVERY 1IN/2.5CM) AND STITCH SLOWLY FOR A SMOOTH EDGE. CLIP THE SEAM ALLOWANCE (MIND THE STITCHES!) TO MAKE THE FABRIC SIT BETTER.

7 Fuse the medium weight interfacing to the wrong side of the lining sides and base circle.

8 On the outer section, topstitch the edging fabric close to the seam between the main and edging fabric.

9 Pin then stitch the other short edges of the outer sections, wrong sides together, to create a tube. Repeat with the lining section.

10 Mark the quarter points on the outer circular base and the outer side. Pin the base to the side section, right sides together, pinning the marked points together first, then the gaps in-between. Stitch the base to the sides. When you need to stop to pivot the fabric, leave the needle down to stay on the seam line. Iron this seam well to get a neat finish, then repeat for the lining sides and base.

11 Turn the outer section right side out and slip it inside the lining section, right sides together. Make sure the two bases are snug against each other and the side seams line up. Stitch around the top edge, leaving a 4–5in (10–12.5cm) turning gap, and reverse stitch at either end of the seam.

12 Turn the basket through the opening. Iron thoroughly, turning in the raw edge on the turning gap as you iron. Pin or glue the gap closed using a washable glue stick, then topstitch the top edge of the basket. Fasten off the ends to finish.

----THE HEDGEHOG FAMILY----

Liz Betts

Use this family of three hedgehogs to make a cute addition to your windowsill or shelf. Cut from the same template enlarged to different sizes, the hedgehogs are simple to sew from four fat quarters and look great either individually or in a group.

MATERIALS

- 4 fat quarters of coordinating fabric
- 18 × 20in (46 × 50cm) paper-backed fusible web
- 4 pieces of A3 card
- Toy stuffing

Top Tip

DRAW AROUND ALL THE TEMPLATES BEFORE CUTTING THEM OUT TO ENSURE ALL THE PIECES FIT ON THE FABRIC.

1 Enlarge the body and head and tummy templates (see Templates) by 400% for the large hedgehog, 360% for the medium hedgehog and 300% for the small hedgehog. Glue the templates onto card and cut out following the line.

2 Make 3in (7.5cm), 4in (10cm) and 5in (13cm) square templates from card to use for the spikes.

3 Position the large hedgehog body template onto the bottom left-hand corner of the wrong side of the first fat quarter and draw around it. Flip the template over and draw around it again, very close to the first drawn body piece. Repeat with the second fat quarter and medium template, then the third fat quarter and small template.

4 Draw around the square templates in the spaces in the fat quarters; above the body

sections and in-between the nose. You will need six of each size in total.

5 Following the manufacturer's instructions, iron the paper-backed fusible web to the wrong side of the fourth fat quarter. Take the head and tummy template for the large hedgehog and draw around it, again close to the edge in the bottom left-hand corner. Flip it over and draw around it again, making sure the templates are close together. Repeat with the medium and small head sections.

6 Cut out all the pieces. Place the squares into piles by size and match up the small, medium and large body and tummy pieces.

7 Take the pieces for the large hedgehog. Peel the paper off the tummy sections then line up along the bottom of the hedgehog and fuse onto the main body. Repeat with the medium and small hedgehogs.

Top Tip

MAKE SURE YOU FLIP THE TEMPLATE, AS THE HEDGEHOG NEEDS TWO OPPOSITE SIDES.

8 Stitch over the join where the tummy section has been fused, by either machine sewing a zigzag stitch or by hand sewing a blanket stitch.

9 Fold the squares in half diagonally and iron. Fold them in half again and iron to make a prairie point. Repeat with all the squares to make the spikes that go along the back of the hedgehogs.

10 Take the small hedgehog and the smallest prairie points. Line up the raw edge of the prairie points along the outside curve of the body. Make sure the open ends face the same way and tuck the prairie points inside each other. Start positioning them from the head across the body, making sure they stop at least ¼in (6mm) before the bottom, and pin them into place.

11 Tack (baste) along the curve, about ⅛in (3mm) from the edge. Trim any of the ends of the prairie points level with the curve.

12 Lay the other section on top, right sides together, and sew a ¼in (6mm) seam allowance along the curve from the nose to the bottom. Sew along the bottom edge of the hedgehog, leaving a 2½in (6.5cm) turning gap in the centre.

13 Make the box corner. At the end of the curve, where the square shape is cut out, pull the two sides of the hedgehog in opposite directions until the seam lies flat. Sew across this line using a ¼in (6mm) seam allowance.

14 Trim the seam allowance to ⅛in (3mm) around the nose. Turn right side out, pushing the corners out and shaping the triangles.

15 Repeat Steps 10–14 to sew the medium and large hedgehogs, then fill the hedgehogs with toy stuffing, pushing in a small amount at a time. Sew the opening closed using a ladder stitch or slipstitch. Make the eyes by sewing on buttons, using scraps of felt or embroidering them.

----SPOTTY DOTTY APRON----

Cynthia Shaffer

Go dotty for this versatile print apron that can be worn either at full length or as a skirt with the bib panel folded under. Complete with pretty pink ribbon tie and a handy pocket for recipes and utensils, you are sure to be the most stylish chef in the kitchen!

MATERIALS

◆ 4 fat quarters of coordinating fabric: red large print, red with white dots, light blue with white dots, pink with white dots

◆ PATTERN NOTES

Seam allowance is ½in (1.2cm), unless stated otherwise

1 Cut a 19 × 20in (48 × 50cm) panel from red large print fabric and a 13 × 20in (33 × 50cm) panel from light blue fabric. With right sides together, stitch the panels together along the long edges.

2 Cut a 31 × 4in (79 × 10cm) panel from the pink fabric – you will need to piece this together to get the 31in (79cm) length.

3 With right sides together, stitch the pink panel to the bottom of the red/light blue panel. Hem the sides and bottom edge by ironing them in by ¼in (6mm), then again by ¼in (6mm), and machine stitching them in place. Fold this panel in half widthways and mark the centre front at the cut edge.

4 For the pocket, cut out an 11 × 6½in (28 × 16.5cm) panel from the light blue fabric and an 11 × 4in (28 × 10cm) panel from the pink fabric. With right sides facing, stitch the panels together along the long edges.

5 Iron the top edge of the pink panel under by ½in (1.2cm), then again by 1in (2.5cm), and stitch the hem in place. Iron the sides and bottom edges under by ½in (1.2cm).

6 Pin the pocket to the apron, 4in (10cm) down from the top edge. Align the right edge with the centre of the apron, which will be 3in (7.5cm) from the red and blue dot seam line. Stitch the pocket in place.

7 Using the red and white dot fabric, cut the apron bib template (see Templates) and transfer the waist centre front mark. To make the hem, iron the top edge under by ¼in (6mm), then again by ¼in (6mm), and stitch in place.

8 Cut two 1½ × 20in (4 × 50cm) strips from the red large print fabric and two 1½ × 13in (4 × 33cm) strips from the pink fabric. Stitch a red and a pink strip together at one short end, then repeat for the second set. Iron the strips in half lengthways, then iron the outer edges in to the fold to create two strips of binding.

9 Stitch the binding to the apron bib sides, matching the seam line of the red and pink fabrics with the top edge of the apron bib. Continue stitching up the binding to form the neck ties.

Top Tip

SERGE OR ZIGZAG THE SEAMS AFTER THEY HAVE BEEN STITCHED, OR USE PINKING SHEARS.

10 With right sides facing and matching the centre front marks, pin and then stitch the bib to the lower apron portion. Iron the seam allowance down towards the apron. Turn the seam allowance under by ¼in (6mm) and stitch in place.

11 Cut four 2 x 20in (5 x 50cm) strips from the pink fabric. Stitch two of the strips together to make a 2 x 40in (5 x 100cm) strip and repeat. With right sides facing, stitch the strip along the long edges and then across one of the short edges to create a long tie. Turn the tie right sides out and iron flat, then stitch it to the apron sides.

----FLORAL DRAWSTRING BAG----

Louise Horler

This lovely drawstring bag makes an ideal sports kit bag for a school child or can be
used as a shoe bag for trips to the gym; simply alter the fabric to suit the recipient.
The drawstring cord is run through a fabric loop to keep it in position.

MATERIALS

- ◆ 4 fat quarters of fabric: 2 of main fabric, 2 of lining fabric
- ◆ 4in (10cm) length of ribbon
- ◆ 1¾yd (1.6m) length of piping cord

◆ PATTERN NOTES
Seam allowance is ⅜in (1cm)

1 Cut a 17½ × 15in (45 × 38cm) rectangle from each fat quarter.

2 Place a main fabric rectangle pattern side up and lay a lining fabric rectangle on top, pattern side down. Pin and machine sew along the top edge, then iron the seam open. Repeat with the remaining pieces of fabric.

3 Position one of the long rectangular pieces of fabric pattern side up, with the main fabric at the bottom and the lining fabric at the top. Fold the ribbon in half to make a loop and place it face down on the right-hand side of the main fabric, about 3in (7.5cm) from the bottom, to make the loop for the cord. The ribbon ends should slightly overhang the edge of the fabric. Place the other large rectangle

of fabric face down on top, making sure that the main fabric and lining fabric pieces match up.

4 Starting at the top left-hand side, pin around the edge of the bag, making sure the ribbon loop is secured in place. Leave a ¾in (2cm) gap for the cord to go through on the right-hand side of the main fabric pieces.

5 Measure 1½in (4cm) down from the top of the main fabric and insert a pin horizontally. Measure ¾in (2cm) down again and insert another pin. This is the gap for the cord and should not be sewn across.

6 Starting at the top left of the lining fabric, sew down to the bottom of the main fabric, across the bottom of the main fabric and

back up to the top of the lining fabric. Leave the gap marked with pins and sew some reinforcing stitches at the start and finish. Do not sew across the top of the lining fabric. Iron the side seams open.

7 Push the bag right sides out through the open end of the lining fabric. Push out the corners using your fingers or a wooden stick if necessary, and iron the main and lining fabric flat. Fold under ½in (1.2cm) of the lining fabric at the bottom of the bag on both sides and iron. Machine sew near to the edge to neatly close the bag lining.

8 Push the lining fabric back inside the main bag, poking the lining corners fully into the corners of the main casing. Iron again.

9 Position pins in the opening on the right-hand side of the bag as a guide, and sew two parallel lines around the top and bottom of the gap to create a channel.

10 Using a safety pin, thread the cord through the gap, around the channel and out the other side. There should be enough cord hanging down on each side to thread through the loop you have made. Tie a knot in the cord, cut off any excess and pull to tighten.

STRIKING POCKET ORGANIZER

Kevin Kosbab

This dazzling pocket organizer is perfect for storing all your paperwork. Hang it using decorative or concealed hardware of your choice: the extra slack in the hanging sleeve will accommodate the thickness of a hanging rod or slat without making the front bulge.

MATERIALS

- 4 fat quarters of fabric
- 18in (46cm) light to medium weight fusible interfacing
- 11 x 15in (28 x 38cm) wadding (batting)

♦ PATTERN NOTES

Seam allowance is ¼in (6mm)

1 Designate the fat quarters as fabrics A–D (A will be the top panel; D will be the lowest panel). Cut 10 x 7¼in (25 x 18.5cm) front panels from fabrics A and D and 10 x 10½in (25 x 27cm) front panels from fabrics B and C.

2 Cut a 10 x 4in (25 x 10cm) back panel from each fabric. From fabric A also cut a 10 x 3½in (25 x 8.5cm) hanging sleeve.

3 From the fusible interfacing cut two 9½ x 6¾in (24 x 17cm) and two 9½ x 10in (24 x 25cm) pieces. Centre each piece onto the wrong side of one of the front panels and fuse in place following the manufacturer's instructions.

4 To construct the organizer front (see Fig 1) first fold 3½in (9cm) to the wrong side along the top edge of panels B, C and D.

5 Open the folds. In order from fabrics A–D, sew the adjacent panels with right sides together along the 10in (25cm) edges. Iron the seams.

6 Refold one of the pockets along the ironed crease and topstitch just these folded layers, about ⅛in (3mm) from the fold. Repeat to topstitch the folded upper edges of the remaining pocket panels. The seams will be the bottom edges of the pockets.

7 To make the organizer back, sew the back panels together along the 10in (25cm) edges, in order from fabrics A–D. Iron the seam allowances open.

8 Centre the sewn back panels right side up on the wadding and pin in place. Topstitch about ⅛in (3mm) to the side of each seam to secure the backing to the wadding. Trim the excess wadding flush with the fabric. The overall backing should measure 10 x 14½in (25 x 37cm).

9 Fold and iron ⅜in (1cm) under at each short end of the hanging sleeve and then iron another ⅜in (1cm) under at each end. Topstitch about ¼in (6mm) from the fold to hem the ends.

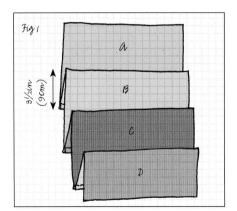

Fig 1

3½in (9cm)

a

B

C

D

10 Iron the hanging sleeve lengthways, 1½in (4cm) from one long edge; there will be more fabric on one side of the fold than the other. With the narrower portion against the backing, align both raw edges of the sleeve with the raw top edge of the backing, centred side to side. Tack (baste) the raw edges. Making sure the narrower portion of the sleeve remains flat against the backing, topstitch along its folded edge to secure the lower edge of the sleeve to the backing.

11 Place the organizer front and backing right sides together, with the pockets on the front panel folded along all creases and seams so they line up with the seams of the backing. Pin together around all edges.

12 Sew the layers together with a generous ¼in (6mm) seam allowance, leaving a 7in (18in) turning gap in the lower edge. Clip the corners to reduce bulk, turn the organizer right sides out through the opening, and gently push out the corners. Iron the outer edges, making sure you iron in the seam allowances at the opening.

13 Topstitch about ⅛in (3mm) inside the edge around the organizer, closing the opening.

----PRETTY PATCHWORK SKIRT----

Liz Betts

This cute patchwork skirt is designed to fit an average seven-year-old, but it can be easily adjusted for girls of six to eight years. Although made from cotton, it is lined, so it would make a warm winter skirt when worn with tights and boots.

MATERIALS

- ◆ 4 fat quarters of fabric
- ◆ 16 × 41in (40 × 102cm) lightweight cotton lining fabric
- ◆ 1in (2.5cm) wide elastic to fit the child's waist – 22½in (56cm) length used here

◆ PATTERN NOTES

Seam allowance is ½in (1.2cm). All seams are ironed open. Seam allowances should be neatened using pinking sheers, a zigzag stitch or overlock stitch

Top Tip

TO MAKE THE SKIRT DURABLE USE THE REVERSE BUTTON ON YOUR SEWING MACHINE TO MAKE A COUPLE OF BACKSTITCHES AT THE START AND FINISH OF EACH LINE.

1 Following Fig 1, cut the following:
FABRIC A: one 9 × 10in (23 × 25cm) rectangle, three 5in (13cm) squares, five 3in (7.5cm) squares, five 3 × 4in (7.5 × 10in) rectangles.
FABRIC B: two 9 × 10in (23 × 25cm) rectangles, one 5in (13cm) square, four 3in (7.5cm) squares, four 3 × 4in (7.5 × 10cm) rectangles.

FABRIC C: one 9 × 10in (23 × 25cm) rectangle, three 5in (13cm) squares, five 3in (7.5cm) squares, six 3 × 4in (7.5 × 10cm) rectangles.
FABRIC D: one 9 × 10in (23 × 25cm) rectangle, three 5in (13cm) squares, six 3in (7.5cm) squares, five 3 × 4in (7.5 × 10cm) rectangles.

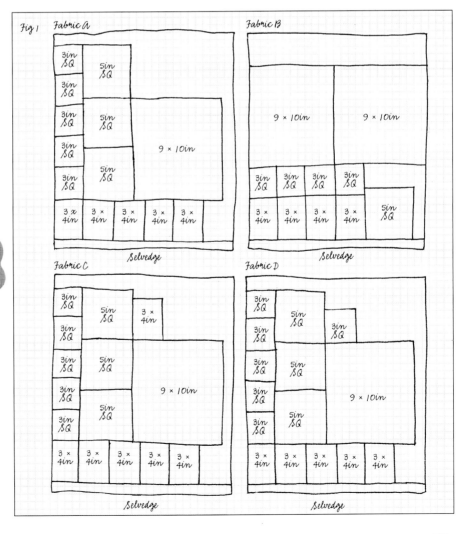

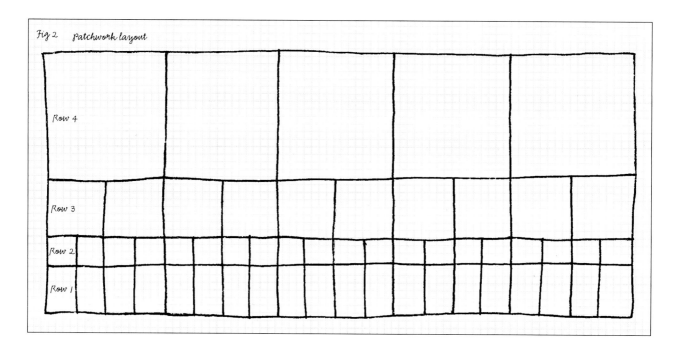

Fig 2   Patchwork layout

Row 4

Row 3

Row 2

Row 1

2 Lay out the fabric in the following rows, alternating the colours (see Fig 2):

ROW 1: Twenty 3 × 4in (7.5 × 10cm) rectangles.

ROW 2: Twenty 3in (7.5cm) squares.

ROW 3: Ten 5in (13cm) squares.

ROW 4: Five 9 × 10in (23 × 25cm) rectangles.

3 Sew the pieces together to make four rows. The completed size of the top row is 10 × 40½in (25 × 101cm) and the bottom row is 4 × 40½in (10 × 101cm).

4 Lay out the rows in the order shown in Fig 2 and sew together. Place pins at the beginning and end of each row and at the fabric intersections to help to align them.

5 Fold the patchwork in half, right sides together, and sew up the shorter side to make a tube. Repeat with the lining fabric.

6 Turn the skirt inside out to the wrong sides to make the casing. At the top (with the large rectangles) fold ¼in (6mm) of fabric to the wrong side and iron. Then fold over another 1¼in (3cm) and iron. Pin into place.

7 Slip the lining over the skirt so the wrong sides are together. Tuck the top of the lining ½in (1.2cm) under the casing and pin into place. Sew along the casing, about ⅛in (3mm) away from the folded edge. Stop sewing approximately 2in (5cm) before your starting point.

8 Measure the child's waist and cut the elastic to this length. Attach a safety pin to one end of the elastic and carefully feed it through the casing. Once it is through, gently gather the fabric away from the ends of the elastic. Overlap the ends by 1in (2.5cm) and pin (for a looser fit, do not overlap so much). Sew over the join, stitching a rectangle with a cross through the centre to secure.

9 Place the elastic under the casing and sew along the hem, starting from just before the place the line of stitching stopped and finishing just over the place that it started.

10 To hem the skirt, fold the raw edge up by ½in (1.2cm) and iron. Turn up another 1in (2.5cm), iron and sew to make a hem. Repeat to hem the lining, ensuring that it is at least ½in (1.2cm) shorter than the skirt.

Top Tip

THE HEM CAN BE MADE WIDER OR NARROWER ACCORDING TO THE CHILD'S HEIGHT.

CRAFTER'S TREASURE BUCKET

Cynthia Shaffer

Every crafter will have a stash of their favourite yarns, fabrics, needles, hooks and pins. Now these treasured items can be stored together in this must-have bucket – complete with sturdy base, strap and generous side pockets – all crafted from four stylish fat quarters.

MATERIALS

- 4 fat quarters of fabric: 1 for outer, 1 for lining, 2 for pockets
- 18in (46cm) fusible pellon
- 18in (46cm) heavyweight fusible interfacing
- 1in (2.5cm) silver overall buckle
- 36in (91.5cm) white cotton strapping, 1in (2.5cm) wide
- 2yd (1.8m) length of white double-wide seam binding

◆ PATTERN NOTES
Seam allowance is ½in (1.2cm)

1 Cut a 22 × 12½in (55 × 32cm) and an 8½ × 12½in (22 × 32cm) panel from the fat quarter of the outer fabric. Stitch the panels together, right sides facing, along the 12½in (32cm) edges and iron the seams flat.

2 Place the panel from Step 1 on top of the fusible pellon and cut around. Fuse the pellon to the wrong side of the panel, following the manufacturer's instructions.

3 Repeat Steps 1 and 2 for the lining fabric.

4 Using the template (see Templates) cut out two pockets from one of the pocket fabrics, two pockets from the other pocket fabric and four pockets from the heavyweight fusible interfacing. Following the manufacturer's instructions, fuse the interfacing to the wrong side of the pocket pieces. Bind the top edges (with the convex curves) with white binding.

5 Pin the pockets to the bottom edge of the outer bucket panel, alternating the fabric patterns. Pin the first pocket 1¼in (3cm) from the left edge, aligning the bottom edges. Pin the right pocket edge parallel to the left pocket edge. The pocket will bulge out away from the panel.

6 Position the next pocket 1¾in (4.5cm) from the first, aligning the bottom edges, and pin the edges in place. Repeat for the two remaining pockets, placing the last one 1¼in (3cm) from the right side of the bucket panel. Sew the pockets in place; stitching down one side, pivoting at the bottom and stitching up the remaining side. Reverse stitch at the start and end of your sewing.

7 With right sides facing, stitch the side seam of the bucket. Repeat for the lining and iron the seams. Slip the lining with right sides out into the outer bucket with wrong sides out, matching the top edges and side seams. Pin in place and stitch together. Turn the bucket so the lining is on the outside, pin the layers together at the bottom and stay stitch them in place.

8 To make the base, draw two 9¼in (23.5cm) diameter circles on the leftover fabric and one on the fusible pellon, either using a pair of compasses or a pencil tied to a piece of string. Fuse the pellon to the wrong side of one of the base pieces. Layer the other bottom piece on top of the pellon, pin the layers and stay stitch together. Pin the base to the outer bucket and stitch the layers together.

9 Using the remaining white binding, bind off the base and bucket seam. Flip the bucket right sides out.

10 Iron and then stitch around the top edge, ¼in (6mm) away from the top. Fold the top down by 1½in (4cm) and iron into place.

11 To make the strap cut a 1¼ × 36in (3.5 × 91.5cm) strip of fabric – you will need to piece this together to get the length. Iron the edges under by ¼in (6mm), centre the strip onto the cotton strapping and stitch into place.

12 Slip the strap into one of the pockets, 6½in (16.5cm) from the folded top edge. Pin and then stitch in place. Slip the overall buckle onto the opposite end of the cotton strap. Following the manufacturer's instructions set the overall button through all the layers, exactly opposite to where the strap goes into the pocket. Hook the overall buckle onto the overall button and adjust the strap as desired.

SUNNY DAY CAMISOLE TOP

Louise Horler

This pretty camisole top is perfect for wearing whilst lounging in a deckchair on a hot day. Easy to make by cutting the armholes from two fat quarters, seaming together and adding binding and tie straps, it is sure to become a staple of your summer wardrobe.

MATERIALS

- 4 fat quarters of fabric in coordinating colours: 1 for front, 1 for back, 2 for bias binding
- 2 pieces of 8½in (22cm) length, ¾in (2cm) width elastic

1 Place the armhole patterns (see Templates) on the top left and top right corners of the front and back fat quarters and cut around.

2 To make the elastic casing, fold the top of the fabric over by ⅜in (1cm) towards the back and iron. Fold over another 1in (2.5cm) and iron again. Machine stitch close to the edge along the bottom of the casing, making reinforcing stitches at the beginning and end.

3 Use a safety pin to thread the elastic through the casing. Hold the end of the elastic at the end of the casing on the right-hand side and stitch up and down to keep it in place. Repeat at the left-hand side to make a gathered top band. Repeat on the other side.

4 Sew the sides using a French seam. Place the fabric pieces together with the pattern on both sides facing outwards. Pin from the bottom of the armhole to the bottom of the fabric and machine sew close to the edge. Repeat on the other side.

5 Turn the top inside out and iron. Machine sew from the bottom of the armhole to the bottom of the fabric, this time using a ⅜in (1cm) seam allowance.

6 To make bias binding for the arm straps, fold one of the remaining fat quarters diagonally in half and iron. Cut along this line and use as a guide to measure, then cut 2in (5cm) wide strips of fabric. You will need approximately 41½in (105cm) of bias binding for each strap.

7 Cut all the short ends of the strips to make sure they are straight. Place one strip horizontally, pattern side up, and another strip on top, pattern side down, at a 90 degree angle. Sew across the overlapping square diagonally from left to right (see Fig 1). Cut off the excess fabric triangle and open the fabric up to form a continuous strip of bias binding. Turn over the binding and iron any seams open.

Top Tip

PIECE SOME STRIPS TOGETHER TO GET THE LENGTH OF THE BIAS BINDING.

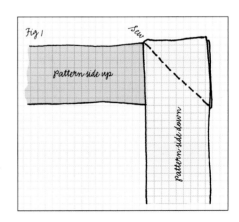

Fig 1

pattern side up

Sew

pattern side down

8 Fold the binding in half lengthways and iron. Open up and fold each side into the middle and iron again. To finish, fold in half and iron again.

9 Make two pieces of the same length for the ties and find the middle point. Starting at the middle of the armhole, sandwich the fabric between the bias binding and pin. Pin up each side of the armhole until you reach the top of each strap end. Machine sew from the top of the strap down along the armhole and up to the other end of the strap. Repeat for the other side of the top.

10 Repeat Steps 6–8 to make 41in (104cm) more bias binding from the final fat quarter. Sandwich the bottom of the top in the bias binding and pin around, then machine sew, slightly overlapping at one of the seams for a neat finish.

----DELIGHTFUL PATCHWORK CUSHION----

Ali Burdon

This pastel print cushion cover with patchwork stripe details would make a charming adornment for a bedroom chair. The finished cover measures 11 × 18in (28 × 46cm), as recommended for a 12 × 20in (30 × 50cm) cushion pad.

MATERIALS

- 5 fat quarters of fabric in coordinating colours: 1 for the main body, 3 for the patchwork sections, binding and lining the cushion top, 1 for the backing section
- 13 × 20in (33 × 50cm) piece of wadding (batting)
- 10in (25cm) of medium weight iron-on interfacing
- 12 × 20in (30 × 50cm) cushion pad

◆ PATTERN NOTES

Seam allowance is ¼in (6cm)

1 Cut four 3½ × 11¾in (9 × 29.5cm) strips from the main body fabric. Now cut five 2½ × 2¾in (6.5 × 7cm) panels from each of the patchwork fabrics (the longer side should be parallel with the selvedge).

2 Cut a 13 × 20in (33 × 50cm) piece for the front lining (this will not be visible, so use any of the fat quarters or plain fabric as an alternative). Now cut a 4 × 11¾in (10 × 29.5cm) piece from any fabric for binding the back section. Cut four 11 × 11¾in (28 × 29.5cm) pieces for the backing and two pieces of the same size from medium weight iron-on interfacing.

3 Arrange the patchwork pieces in three columns of five pieces, with the shorter edges at the top and bottom (see Fig 1). Stitch the three columns together and then iron all the seams open.

4 Stitch the strips of the main body fabric to the patchwork sections, alternating the two, and starting and finishing with a strip of main body fabric. Iron the seams open.

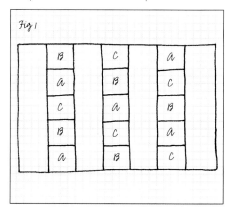

Fig 1

B	C	A
A	B	C
C	A	B
B	C	A
A	B	C

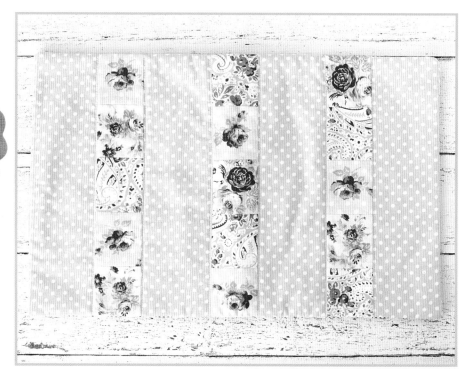

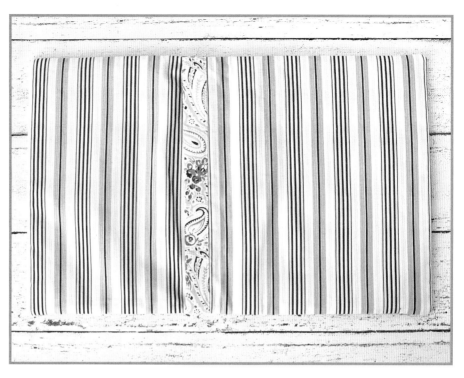

5 Lay the 13 × 20in (33 × 50cm) piece of cushion top lining fabric wrong side up on your work surface, then place the wadding on top. Position the cushion top right side up on top of the wadding and pin together. Quilt the cushion top, making a line of stitching on either side of each patchwork section. Trim off the excess wadding and lining fabric.

6 Apply interfacing to two of the backing pieces, following the manufacturer's instructions. Place an interfaced and a non-interfaced piece wrong sides together and stitch along one of the 11¾in (29.5cm) edges. Turn right side out, iron and then topstitch the seam.

7 Make the binding by folding the 4 × 11¾in (10 × 29.5cm) piece lengthways and finger pressing to make a crease. Fold the outer edges in towards the crease and then iron.

8 Place the remaining two backing pieces wrong sides together. Unfold one edge of the binding, line it up with one of the 11¾in (29.5cm) edges and pin in place. Stitch along the first fold line on the binding, about 1in (2.5cm) down from the raw edges. Fold the binding over the raw edges and to the back, iron well and slipstitch into place. Topstitch the binding edge.

9 Place the cushion top right side up on your work surface. Place the bound backing section right sides together with it; the raw edge should align with the right-hand raw edge of the cushion top. Then place the backing section with the seamed edge on the other side. Pin and stitch around the edge of the cushion. Clip across the corners and zigzag stitch the raw edges. Sew extra zigzag stitches where the two backing sections overlap for extra strength.

10 Turn the cushion cover right side out and push out the corners with a wooden stick or similar. Insert the cushion pad to finish.

Top Tip
YOU CAN ADD MORE QUILTING TO THE CUSHION TOP, IF DESIRED.

----FARM POCKETS PLAYMAT----

Jo Avery

This fun farm-themed playmat – complete with brightly coloured patchwork tractor and trailer, barn and apple tree – will delight your little ones. Each block features a secret pocket that can be filled with toy animals for a special finishing touch.

MATERIALS

- 6 fat quarters of fabric: blue, turquoise, red, yellow, green, brown
- 34in (86.5cm) square of wadding (batting)
- 34in (86.5cm) square of backing fabric
- Binding: 7in (18cm) from a full width of fabric
- Scraps of felt and fabric

◆ PATTERN NOTES

Seam allowance is ¼in (6mm), unless stated otherwise. Try to iron all seams towards the darker side of the fabric. Where appropriate, the blocks will be strip pieced (trimmed to size after they are sewn). Your fat quarter will have one side slightly shorter/longer than the other; follow the instructions given for where it is important to cut from a certain side.

1 Cut the following from the fat quarters:
BLUE (short side): three 1½in (4cm) strips, one 2in (5cm) strip and one 4in (10cm) strip – from this cut a 14in (36cm) strip and a 4in (10cm) square. Cut one 8⅞in (23cm) square and from the remainder, cut one each of the following strips: 1in (2.5cm), 1½in (4cm) and 3½in (9cm).

TURQUOISE (short side): one 4½in (11.5cm) strip – from this cut a 7in (18cm) piece, a 2in (5cm) piece, and a 3½ × 8½in (9 × 22cm) rectangle – and one 16½ × 11in (42 × 28cm) rectangle. From the remainder, cut the following strips from the longest side: 1½in (4cm), 2½in (6.5cm) and 3½in (9cm). From the 2½in (6.5cm) piece, cut one 8½in (22cm) strip and one 2 × 8in (5 × 20cm) rectangle.

GREEN (long side): one 11½in (29cm) strip – from this cut an 11½in (29cm) square. From the remainder cut one of the following: 2½in (6.5cm) strip, 1½in (4cm) strip and 6 × 3in (15 × 7.5cm) rectangle. Now cut one 5½ × 14in (14 × 35.5cm) rectangle, one 1½in (4cm) strip and one 4in (10cm) square.

RED: one 8⅞in (23cm) square and one 5in (12.5cm) strip.

YELLOW (long side): one 6in (15cm) strip – from this cut a 6½in (16.5cm) piece. Cut the following strips: two 4½in (11.5cm), one 1½in (4cm), one 4in (10cm) – from this cut one 5in (12.5cm) piece. Cut the remainder of the strip down to 3½in (9cm) and cut one 6in (15cm) length, one 2½in (6.5cm) length and two 2in (5cm) lengths, all for the hay bales. For the pockets cut two 2½ × 3½in (6.5 × 9cm) rectangles.

BROWN: one 7½in (19cm), one 5½in (14cm) square, one 1½in (4cm) strip, two 6½in (16.5cm) squares, one 4½ × 6in (11.5 × 15cm) rectangle and one 6 × 9in (15 × 23cm) rectangle.

BINDING: Cut four 1½in (4cm) strips.

2 To make the barn block, fold over one of the 6½in (16.5cm) brown squares on the longest side and iron. Pin to the matching brown square, right sides together, so the folded edge sits in the centre and the raw edges line up together at the left hand side. Sew together at the left hand side to make the door pocket, keeping the pins in place for now. Sew along the bottom edge using a ⅛in (3mm) seam.

3 Sew 4½in (11.5cm) yellow strips to each side and trim to match the door. Sew a yellow 1½in (4cm) strip to the top and a 1½in (4cm) blue strip to each side (see Fig 1).

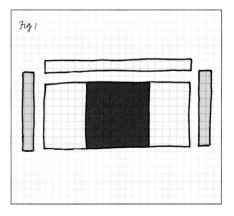
Fig 1

4 Cut the 8⅞in (23cm) red square in half diagonally and repeat with the blue 8⅞in (23cm) square. Sew a red triangle to a blue triangle and repeat to make two squares. Sew together to make the roof, then sew a 1½in (4cm) blue strip on top (see Fig 2). Sew the roof to the barn.

5 To make the apple tree block, fold over the 6 × 9in (15 × 23cm) brown rectangle on the longest side and iron. Pin this to the 4½ × 6in (11.5 × 15cm) brown rectangle, right sides together, so the folded edge sits on the left and the raw edges line up together at the right-hand side. Sew together at the right-hand side to make the tree trunk pocket, keeping the pins in place for now. Sew along the bottom edge with a ⅛in (3mm) seam.

6 Sew the 6 × 6½in (15 × 16.5cm) yellow rectangles at either side of the tree trunk and the 16½ × 11in (42 × 28cm) turquoise rectangle to the top (see Fig 3).

7 Fold your large green square into four quarters and use a pair of compasses or a pencil tied to a string to cut a out a circle with a 12in (30cm) diameter. Cut out a matching circle from scrap fabric. Pin right sides together and sew around the circumference. Make a small slit in the scrap fabric and turn inside out. Turn the lined circle out fully and iron. Pin to the top of the tree trunk and topstitch close to the edge with matching thread. Carefully cut away the excess turquoise thread from behind the treetop and set aside.

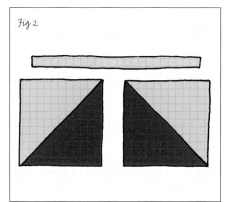

Fig 2

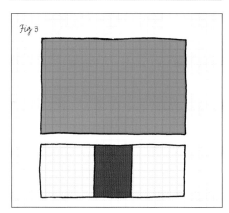

Fig 3

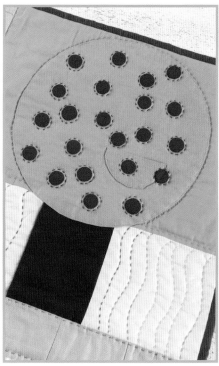

8 Draw and cut out a 4in (10cm) circle from green fabric for the tree pocket, then fold in half and iron. Stitch around the curved edge to partially close the semi-circle, leaving a 1½in (4cm) gap. Turn inside out and iron. Fold in the seams at the opening and pin closed. Pin the pocket to the tree then topstitch the bottom curved edge, close to the edge, closing the gap at the same time.

9 Draw and cut out 22 circles of 1in (2.5cm) diameter from red felt for the apples. Pin all over the treetop and stitch in place.

10 To make the tractor block, take the large green rectangle and sew the largest remaining turquoise rectangle beneath it. Take a 1½in (4cm) turquoise strip and cut a 1½in (4cm) square from one end. Sandwich part of a 1½in (4cm) brown strip between the turquoise strip and square. Trim the brown strip and sew to the right-hand side of the tractor bottom (see Fig 4).

11 From turquoise fabric cut a 6½ × 4in (16.5 × 10cm) rectangle for the sky and cut a diagonal from the top right-hand corner,

to about a third of the way along the bottom edge. Now cut a 5 × 3½in (13 × 9cm) rectangle from green fabric for the cab and cut a diagonal from the bottom left corner.

12 Sew green 1½in (4cm) strips to the top, the left-hand side and the bottom of the cab. Trim the strips in line with the angled edge of the tractor cab. Sew a green 1½in (4cm) strip to the angled tractor cab side and sew the tractor sky piece to this (see Fig 5).

13 Sew the remaining turquoise strips to the tractor cab rectangle (see Fig 6).

14 Sew the tractor cab to the tractor bottom and stitch a 1½in (4cm) strip to the left-hand side of the block (see Fig 7).

15 Fold the 6 × 3in (15 × 7.5cm) green fabric rectangle in half and sew around three sides, with right sides together, to make the pocket. Turn inside out; fold the opening seams in, iron and pin closed. Pin this pocket to the door position on the tractor, with the opening at the bottom. Topstitch close to the edge around three sides with matching thread, leaving the top open.

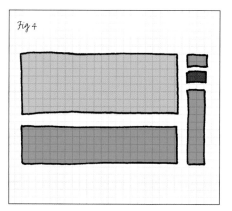

Fig 4

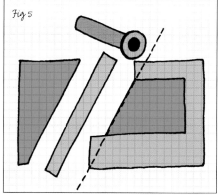

Fig 5

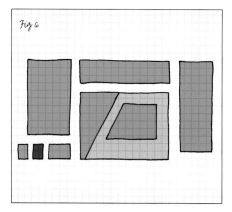

Fig 6

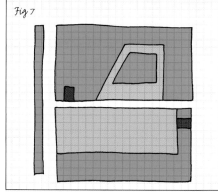

Fig 7

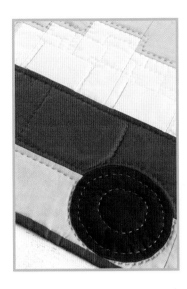

16 For the tractor wheels, fold the large brown square into four quarters and cut a 7½in (19cm) diameter circle. Cut out a matching circle from scrap fabric. Pin with right sides together and sew around the circumference. Make a small slit in the scrap fabric and turn inside out. Turn the lined circle out fully and iron. Cut a 5½in (14cm) circle from brown fabric and repeat. Pin the wheels in place and topstitch close to the edge.

17 To make the hay bale block, sew the remaining large blue rectangle to the large red rectangle. Sew a 1½in (4cm) blue strip to the right-hand side of this block (see Fig 8).

18 Sew your yellow hay rectangles onto the corresponding blue strips (see Fig 9), then sew the strips together. Sew a 1½in (4cm) blue strip to the left hand side and a 2½in (6.5cm) strip to the right hand side of this hay panel.

19 Stitch the red and blue hay bale rectangle to the yellow and blue hay panel. Cut a 6½in (16.5cm) piece from the remaining 2in (5cm) blue strip and sandwich a 1½in (4cm) brown strip between this and the remainder of the strip. Trim the brown strip and sew to the left-hand side of the trailer bottom (see Fig 10).

20 Fold one of the yellow 2½ × 3½in (6.5 × 9cm) pocket rectangles in half and sew around three sides, with right sides together. Turn inside out; fold the opening seams in, then iron and pin closed. Repeat with the other pocket rectangle. Pin these pockets on top of the hay bales with the opening at bottom. With matching thread, topstitch close to the edge around three sides, leaving the top open.

21 Follow Step 16 to make a small wheel from brown fabric, pin in place and topstitch close to the edge.

22 Trim any excess from the blocks: they should now each measure 16½in (42cm) square. Sew the blocks together.

23 Iron the quilt top and backing fabric. Lay the backing fabric right side down on a clean, hard surface and secure the edges in place with masking tape. Layer the wadding followed by the quilt top, right side up. Your backing and wadding should overlap all the way around. Pin through all three layers using safety pins, no more than 4–6in (10–15cm) apart and remove the tape.

24 Hand quilt the playmat using embroidery thread and running stitch. Add details, such as corn, and accentuate features, such as the hay bales and wheels.

25 Sew a 1¾in (4.5cm) binding strip, right sides together, to the top edge of the playmat front using a ⅝in (1.5cm) seam. Trim to fit and sew a second strip to the bottom of the quilt. Repeat with the side edges, sewing from binding to binding edge and trimming to fit. Turn the quilt over and fold the binding around to the back. Fold the raw edge under all the way around and pin, folding in a mitre at the corners. Slipstitch the binding to the back of the quilt with matching thread, making sure you don't sew through to the front of the quilt.

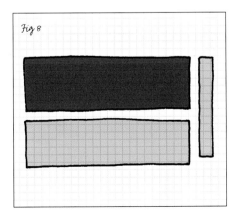

Fig 8

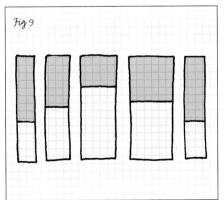

Fig 9

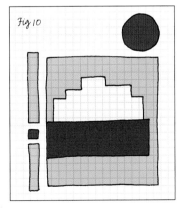

Fig 10

----AUTUMNAL COWL----

Prudence Rogers

When it's not quite cold enough for its knitted cousin, this fabric version of the infinity scarf is the perfect choice. So easy and quick to make, you don't need to stick to the autumnal shades; rustle up several colourways for different days.

MATERIALS

♦ 6 fat quarters of fabric in coordinating colours: 3 darker and 3 lighter (optional)

Top Tip

CHOOSE THREE DARKER AND THREE LIGHTER FABRICS FOR A REVERSIBLE EFFECT OR SUBSTITUTE FOR YOUR FAVOURITE FABRIC COMBINATION.

1 Cut all six fat quarters down to a 21 × 15½in (53.5 × 35.5cm) rectangle.

2 Take two fat quarters (the darker ones if you are having a darker and lighter side), place right sides together, pin and sew along the shorter side with a ½in (1.2cm) seam allowance. Add a third fat quarter in the same way to make a very long rectangle. Iron the seams out flat.

3 Repeat the process for the other three (lighter) fat quarters, so you have two long rectangles, each made from three fat quarters. Take care to match any directional prints.

4 Place the two rectangles on top of each other, right sides facing. Pin and sew seams down each of the long sides using a ½in (1.2cm) allowance. Iron the seams flat.

5 Turn out to the right sides but only pull through to about halfway. Match the two circle ends of the raw edges together as you pull the tube up inside itself, so that the right sides are facing. Match up the seams in each side then twist the inner tube around so that it now matches up to the opposite seam. Pin in place. This gives a twist in the scarf when finished, making it more three-dimensional. Sew around the tube using a ½in (1.2cm) seam allowance to join the two ends together, leaving a 4½in (32cm) gap for turning through (see Fig 1).

6 Using the opening, turn the scarf out to the right sides and tuck in the raw edges of the gap to match the seam. Close the opening, either using neat machine topstitching close to the folded edge or hand sewing with slipstitch.

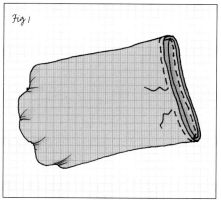

Fig 1

---NATURE NESTING BOWLS----

Emily Levey

These sweet nesting bowls are pretty stacked and displayed together, or they can be used throughout the home for organizing all your bits and bobs. I chose prints featuring ladybirds, flowers and birds and formed the corners into leaf shapes for a nature theme.

MATERIALS

- 6 fat quarters of fabric
- 50cm (20in) square compressed fleece
- 50cm (20in) square iron-on interfacing

◆ PATTERN NOTES
Seam allowance is ½in (1.2cm), unless stated otherwise

1 For the large bowl cut two 19in (48.5cm) squares from fabric, one 19in (48.5cm) square from compressed fleece and one 18in (46cm) square from iron-on interfacing.

2 For the medium bowl cut two 15in (38cm) squares from fabric, one 15in (38cm) square from compressed fleece and one 14in (35.5cm) square from iron-on interfacing.

3 For the small bowl cut two 10in (25cm) squares from fabric, one 10in (25cm) square from compressed fleece and one 9in (23cm) square from iron-on interfacing.

4 For the tiny bowl cut two 6½in (16.5cm) squares from fabric, one 6½in (16.5cm) square from compressed fleece and one 5½in (14cm) square from iron-on interfacing.

5 Use the following steps for each nesting bowl. On the wrong side of one fabric square, fuse the iron-on interfacing for

the inside of the bowl, following the manufacturer's instructions. You should have a 1½in (1.2cm) gap around each edge.

6 Place the other fabric square wrong side down onto the compressed fleece. Now place the fabric square with the interfacing onto this, so that the right sides of the fabric are facing each other. Pin around the outer edges.

7 Sew around all four sides, leaving a 3–4in (7.5–10cm) turning gap on one side. You can use the edge of the interfacing as a guide for your seam allowance. Clip the corners to reduce bulk.

8 Turn the right sides out through the gap, using a wooden stick or similar to push out the corners into a neat point. Iron well and tuck the raw edges of the unsewn gap inside, then iron or pin the gap closed.

9 Topstitch around each side, ⅛in (3mm) from the edge, to close the gap.

10 Repeat step 1-4 with the remaining squares for the other bowl sizes.

11 To form the sides of the bowls, start with the large bowl and fold the square in half diagonally, with the interfaced fabric on the inside. Measure 3in (7.5cm) from the point along the topstitched edge and mark. Sew a line at a 90-degree angle to the topstitched edge, reverse stitching at the start and end to secure. Repeat for the opposite corner (see Fig 1).

12 Open out the triangle and refold diagonally in the other direction. Repeat Step 11 for the two remaining corners.

13 Repeat Steps 11–12, substituting the measurements from the corner as follows: 2½in (6.5cm) for the medium bowl, 2in (5cm) for the small bowl and 1in (2.5cm) for the tiny bowl.

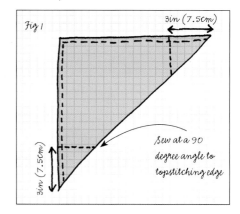

Fig 1

3in (7.5cm)

3in (7.5cm)

Sew at a 90 degree angle to topstitching edge

----RETRO RING PLACEMATS----

Kevin Kosbab

This striking retro-style placemat set will liven up your mealtimes. Simply cut fat quarters on the diagonal and stitch them together with a contrasting fabric, before quilting and binding. The interlocking bias rings add colour and interest to the design.

MATERIALS
(for 2 placemats)

- 6 fat quarters of fabric: 4 solids and 2 prints
- 27in (69cm) square of wadding (batting)
- ⅜in (8mm) bias tape maker

1 Designate the fat quarters as Fabrics A – F. Fabric A (the pearl print in the photograph) will only be used for appliqué; Fabric B (grey polka dot) will be part of the front of each placemat. The other fabrics will be used for various components.

2 Trim any selvages away from the fat quarters and cut each one at a 45-degree angle, starting from one of the corners. Cut one ¾in (2cm) wide bias strip from the wider section of Fabrics E and F and two from the wider section of Fabric A (see Fig 1). Set the bias strips aside.

3 To make the placemat fronts sew a Fabric B triangle to a Fabric C triangle, right sides together along the bias edges, to form a rectangle. Repeat to sew a Fabric B triangle to a Fabric D triangle. To make the placemat backs, sew together triangles of Fabrics D and E, then Fabrics C and F (see Fig 2). Iron the seam allowances towards the darker fabrics.

4 Cut a 17 x 13½in (43 x 34cm) rectangle from each of the placemat fronts, keeping the corner of the cut rectangle on the diagonal seam (see Fig 3). Do not cut the sewn backs.

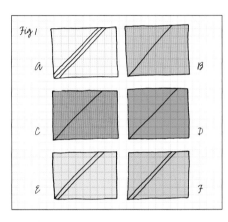

Fig 1

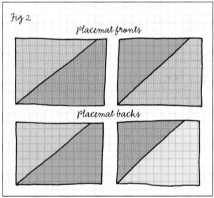

Fig 2

placemat fronts

placemat backs

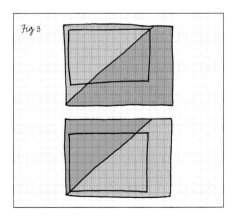

Fig 3

Top Tip
TAKE CARE NOT TO STRETCH THE FABRIC TRIANGLES WHEN YOU SEW THEM TOGETHER.

5 Following the manufacturer's instructions, run each bias strip through the bias tape maker to turn under the edges. Pin a Fabric A bias tape roughly into a round shape on each of the placemat fronts. Trim the excess ends where they meet and place the meeting point where it can be covered with the subsequent ring. Repeat with a contrasting bias tape (Fabric F tape on Fabric C placemat; Fabric E tape on Fabric D placemat), arranging this ring to cover the join in the Fabric A ring, with the ends of the new ring meeting at a point on the Fabric A ring.

6 Hand sew the bias tape edges to the background fabric using small stitches in fine matching thread through the fold of the tape. Alternatively, machine appliqué the tapes with clear monofilament thread and a tiny zigzag stitch, or by topstitching.

7 Cut two 15 × 19in (38 × 48.5cm) rectangles from wadding. Layer the placemat backs wrong side up and spread a wadding rectangle over each. Place a placemat front right side up on each stack (Fabric B/C front with D/E back; Fabric B/D front with C/F back). Ensure the fronts are roughly centred on the wadding and line up the diagonal seams on the fronts and backs. Secure the layers together with safety pins.

8 Quilt each placemat as desired. I quilted straight lines parallel to the diagonal seams using a walking foot and contrasting thread. To give the appliqué dimension, free-motion quilt just outside the bias tapes with thread to match the background.

9 Cut four 2in (5cm) wide bias strips from each of the unused Fabric E and F pieces cut in Step 2. Join the strips of each fabric together and iron the seam allowances open. Now iron each strip in half lengthways, wrong sides together.

10 Bind the Fabric B/C placemat with the strip of Fabric E and the Fabric B/D placemat with the strip of Fabric F. Alternatively, both placemats could be bound with strips of the leftover Fabric A.

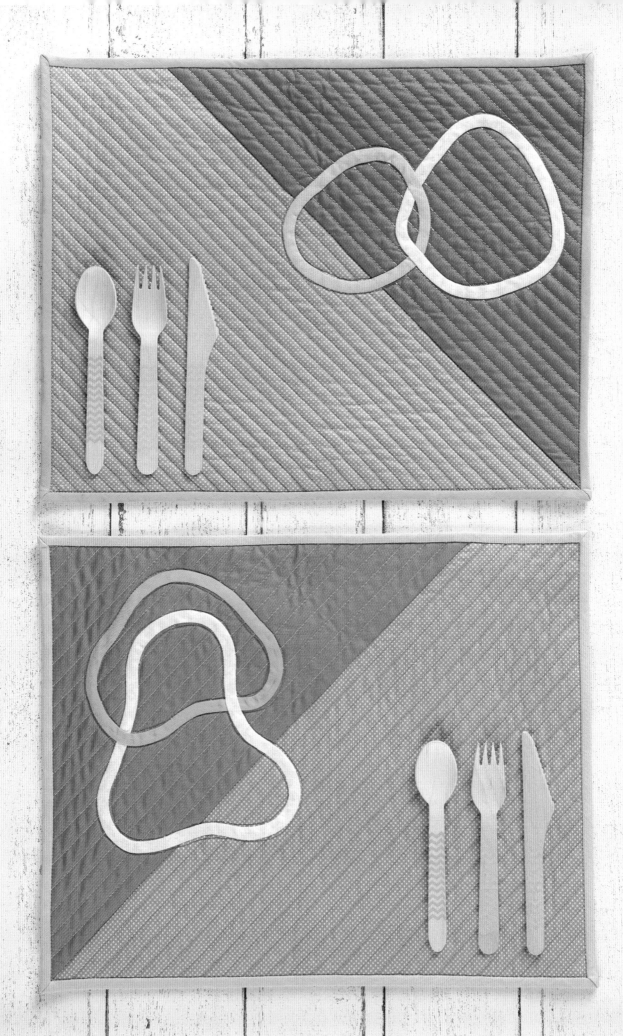

----BIG BOW CLUTCH----

Prudence Rogers

Create a statement with this stylish clutch with oversized bow, created from six fat quarters in three coordinating floral fabrics. With a practical pocket and a magnetic clasp for easy access, this must-have accessory is the perfect introduction to bag making.

MATERIALS

- 6 fat quarters of fabric: 2 each of 3 coordinating designs
- 20in (50cm) heavyweight fusible interfacing
- 20in (50cm) medium weight fusible interfacing
- Magnetic bag clasp

1 Cut two 8 × 12in (20 × 30.5cm) and two 3¼ × 13in (8 × 33cm) rectangles from the main fabric, carefully matching the pattern if necessary. Cut one 3¼ × 26in (8 × 66cm) and two 8 × 12in (20 × 30.5cm) rectangles from the medium weight interfacing.

2 Cut two 7 × 11¼in (18 × 28.5cm) rectangles of heavyweight interfacing and fuse to the wrong side centre of each large main fabric rectangle. Iron the medium weight interfacing onto the top of each piece, sandwiching the heavyweight interfacing in the centre.

3 Place the two narrow rectangles with right sides together and sew down the short edge at one end with a ½in (1.2cm) seam allowance. Open out to make one long strip and iron open the seam. Fuse the remaining strip of medium weight interfacing to the wrong side of the fabric.

4 To form the sides, pin the long strip around three edges of one of the large main fabric rectangles, right sides together. Sew with a ½in (1.2cm) seam allowance (see Fig 1).

5 Pin and sew the other large main fabric rectangle to the strip in the same way and turn right sides out. Trim any excess material from the strip to make it level with the top of the bag (see Fig 2). Attach the back plate of the magnetic fastening in the centre of the front panel, 1½in (4cm) from the bottom, following the manufacturer's instructions.

Top Tip

DON'T WORRY IF THE CORNERS BUNCH UP SLIGHTLY. MAKE YOUR TURN AND SEW A RIGHT-ANGLED CORNER AND WHEN FINISHED, CLIP THE CORNERS TO ALLOW THE SEAM TO LIE FLAT.

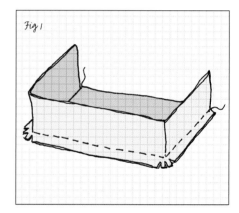

Fig 1

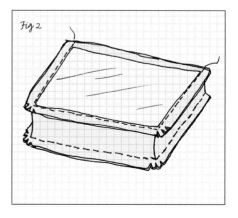

Fig 2

6 To make the lining, cut two 3¼ × 12in (8 × 30.5cm) and two 3¼ × 13in (8 × 33cm) rectangles from the lining fabric, carefully matching the pattern if required. Cut one 3¼ × 26in (8 × 66cm) and two 8 × 12in (20 × 30.5cm) rectangles of medium weight interfacing. Repeat Steps 2 and 3.

7 To make the interior pocket, cut a 7 × 9in (18 × 23cm) rectangle from the third fabric design and fold in half with right sides together. Pin, then sew around the outer edge using a ½in (1.2cm) seam allowance and leaving a 2in (5cm) gap for turning. Clip the corners and turn through to right sides. Fold in the raw edges of the opening and pin to the centre of one of the lining main body pieces with the folded edge at the top. Sew around three sides of the pocket, close to the edge.

8 Sew up the three lining pieces in the same way as for the main body, leaving a 4in (10cm) turning gap. Do not turn right sides out. Place the outer bag inside the lining section and neatly pin around the top raw

edges. Sew around the edge to join, using a ½in (1.2cm) seam allowance. Turn right sides out through the gap in the lining and iron. Slip stitch the gap closed by hand and push back inside the bag, ironing around the top edge to flatten. Topstitch around the top of the bag, ¼in (6mm) from the edge (see Fig 3).

9 For the flap, cut a 12 × 9in (30.5 × 23cm) rectangle from both the main bag fabric and lining fabric, matching the patterns if required. Cut one 11½ × 8½in (29 × 21.5cm) rectangle from the heavyweight interfacing and fuse to the main fabric rectangle. Cut a piece of medium weight interfacing the same size as the flap and fuse over the top, sandwiching the heavyweight interfacing in the centre. Follow the manufacturer's instructions to attach the top of the magnetic fastener, 2in (5cm) from the bottom edge on the lining fabric side of the flap.

10 Place the two flap pieces right sides together and pin and sew around the edge with a ½in (1.2cm) seam allowance, leaving a 3in (7.5cm) turning gap. Clip the corners and turn through to the right sides. Tuck the raw edges of the opening inside, slipstitch closed by hand and iron.

11 Pin the flap to the back of the bag, overlapping the lining by 1in (2.5cm). Check the magnetic fastening parts match and topstitch the flap onto the bag, ¼in (6mm) from the edge (see Fig 4).

12 Fold the centres of each side of the back inwards and hand sew to secure (see Fig 5). Fold the flap over the top and close with the magnetic fastener.

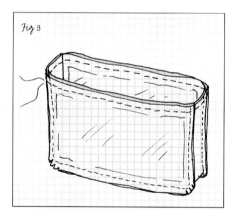

Fig 3

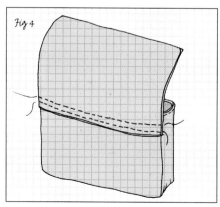

Fig 4

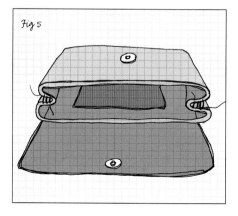

Fig 5

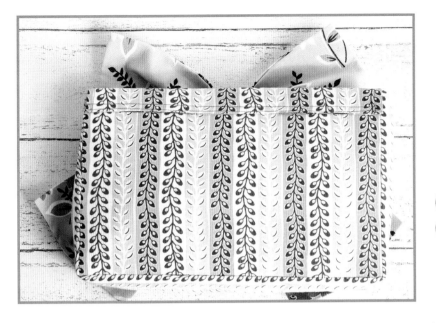

13 To make the bow, cut a 13 × 22in (33 × 56cm) rectangle from the third fabric design and fold in half lengthways with right sides together. Sew up the long edge with a ¼in (6mm) seam allowance to form a tube, iron the seam open and turn right sides out. Iron flat so that the seam is centred on the back. Turn the raw edge at one end inside by ¼in (6mm) and iron into place. Loop the other end of the tube around and put the raw edge inside the end with a fold measuring approximately ¼in (6mm). Pin and topstitch across the tube, being careful not to catch the other side of the loop in the stitching (see Fig 6).

14 Cut a 5 × 17in (13 × 43cm) rectangle from the same fabric. Fold in half with wrong sides together and sew the three open edges with a ¼in (6mm) seam allowance, leaving a 2⅜in (6cm) opening. Clip the corners, turn

through to the right sides and slipstitch the opening closed by hand.

15 Cut a 2⅜ × 6in (6 × 15cm) rectangle from the bow fabric, fold in half lengthways with right sides together, and sew along the long edge with a ¼in (6mm) seam allowance. Turn right sides out, using a wooden stick or similar. Iron flat making sure that the seam is centred at the back.

16 Lie the largest rectangle down and place the fabric loop on top in the centre. Carefully tuck and gather up the central fabric slightly to form a bow shape and wrap the small strip tightly around the middle (see Fig 7). The strip will be too long: pin it into place, then machine stitch the two strips together, as close as you can to the bow. Cut off the excess from the strip, about ¼in (6mm) from the stitching.

17 Hand sew the bow in position. Stitch through the folds and the centre tie to secure.

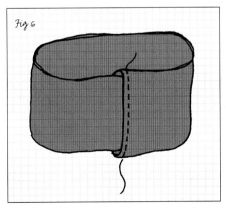

Fig 6

Fig 7

----MINI QUILT WALL HANGING----

Jo Avery

This mini patchwork quilt, pieced together in a unique grid pattern cut from six fat quarters, will make a stunning addition to any room. Simply insert a wooden dowel into the fabric corner panels at the back of the quilt to hang.

MATERIALS

- ◆ 6 fat quarters of fabric: 2 neutral, 1 turquoise, 1 blue, 1 yellow, 1 coral
- ◆ 30in (76cm) square of wadding (batting)
- ◆ 30in (76cm) square of backing fabric

◆ PATTERN NOTES

Seam allowance is ¼in (6mm), unless stated otherwise. Where possible, iron all seams towards the darker side of the fabric.

1 Cut the following from the fat quarters:
NEUTRAL: ten 2½in (6.5cm) and three 3½in (9cm) strips.
CORAL: four 3½in (9cm) strips.
TURQUOISE: three 2½in (6.5cm) strips and two 4⅞in (12.5cm) squares.
BLUE: two 2½in (6.5cm) and six 1¾in (4.5cm) strips.
YELLOW: two 4⅞in (12.5cm), two 4½in (11.5cm) and two 4in (10cm) squares, and a 4½ x 12½in (11.5 x 32cm) rectangle.

2 Take the two neutral strips and cut into eight 4½in (11.5cm) strips.

3 Cut the 4⅞in (12.5cm) squares in half diagonally, match two different colour triangles and sew together to make four 4½in (11.5cm) squares.

4 Sew together two blue strips and two neutral strips. Cut these pieced strips into 16 small strips measuring 2½ x 4½in (6.5 x 11.5cm). Sew two blue and two neutral strips together to form a checkerboard square (see Fig 1). Repeat to make four checkerboard squares.

5 Sew three coral strips to three neutral strips. Cut these pieced strips into twenty 2½ x 4½in (6.5 x 11.5cm) strips and sew eight of these pieces to a 4½in (11.5cm) neutral strip (see Fig 2).

6 Make the centre block by sewing the blue and neutral units together with the yellow 4½in (11.5cm) squares and the yellow rectangle (see Fig 3).

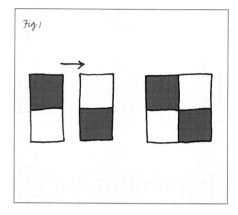

Fig 1

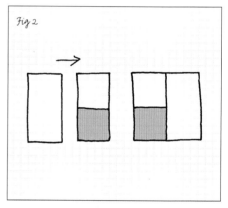

Fig 2

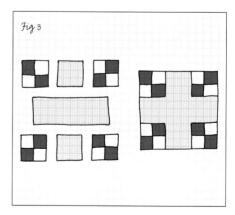

Fig 3

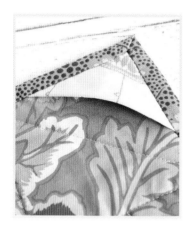

7 Sew the turquoise strips to three neutral strips. Cut these pieced strips into eight 5½ × 4½in (14 × 11.5cm) rectangles. Take the remaining coral strip and sew a 3½in (9cm) neutral strip to either side. Cut these pieced strips into four 8½ × 4½in rectangles. Sew together the coral/neutral and turquoise/neutral units (see Fig 4) to make four side blocks.

8 Sew the remaining blue/neutral and coral/neutral units together with the yellow/turquoise triangular squares to make corner blocks (see Fig 5).

9 Sew a side block to each side of the centre square and a corner block to each corner of a side block (see Fig 6). Sew the three strips together.

10 Iron the quilt top and backing fabric. Place the backing fabric right side down and secure the edges to the surface with masking tape. Layer the wadding on top, followed by the quilt top, right side up. The backing and wadding should overlap all the way around. Pin through all three layers with safety pins no more than 4–6in (10–15cm) apart, and remove the tape.

11 Machine quilt the wall hanging using a grid pattern.

12 Sew together two of the 1¾in (4.5cm) blue strips to form a longer strip. Iron the seams open. With right sides together, sew this strip to the top edge of the quilt front using a ⅝in (1.5cm) seam. Trim the binding strip to fit, sew the remainder to another 1¾in (4.5cm) blue strip and use this to sew to the bottom of your quilt. Repeat with the side edges, sewing from binding to binding edge and trimming to fit.

13 Turn the quilt over and fold the binding around to the back. Fold the raw edge under all the way around and pin, folding in a mitre at the corners.

14 Take the two remaining 4in (10cm) squares and fold in half diagonally. Insert

these at the top corners, between the folded under binding and the back of the quilt, with the raw edges together. Pin through these hangers when pinning the binding down.

15 Slipstitch the binding to the quilt back, sewing through the hanger layers, but not through to the quilt front. Insert a wooden dowel between the corner hangers to hang.

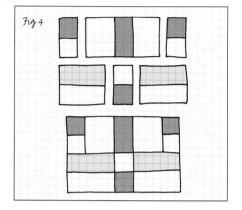

Fig 4

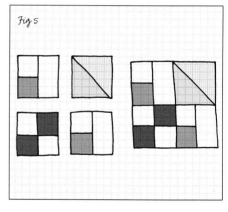

Fig 5

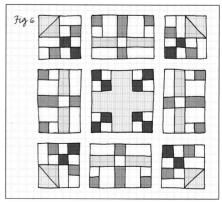

Fig 6

----COOL COLOURBLOCK TOTE----

Kaye Prince

Shop in style with this bright tote bag sewn from panels of bold block colour, complete with a sturdy handle and handy interior pocket. Have fun choosing colours to suit your style and quilting in your own design to make a totally unique tote!

MATERIALS

- 6 fat quarters of fabric
- 18in (46cm) fusible fleece
- 9in (23cm) medium weight interfacing

♦ PATTERN NOTES

Seam allowance is ½in (1.2cm)

1 For the tote outer and interior pocket cut two 8 × 20in (20 × 50cm) rectangles from fat quarter 1 and two 9 × 20in (23 × 50cm) rectangles from fat quarter 2. From fat quarter 3 cut two 4 × 20in (10 × 50cm) rectangles and one 10 × 15in (25 × 38cm) rectangle for the pocket.

2 For the tote lining and handles cut two 8 × 20in (20 × 50cm) rectangles from fat quarter 4, two 9 × 20in (23 × 50cm) rectangles from fat quarter 5 and four 4 × 20in (10 × 50cm) rectangles (two for the handles) from fat quarter 6.

3 Cut two 19 × 20in (48 × 50cm) rectangles from the fusible fleece and two 3½ × 20in (9 × 50cm) rectangles from the interfacing.

4 To piece the outer and lining panels, line up one 8 × 20in (20 × 50cm) rectangle, one 9 × 20in (23 × 50cm) rectangle, and one 4 × 20in (10 × 50cm) rectangle along their long sides. This is the layout for each tote panel: sew these three rectangles together

to form the panel. Repeat for all four panels (outer and lining).

5 To make the interior pocket, fold the 10 × 15in (25 × 38cm) rectangle in half, right sides together, to form a 10 × 7½in (25 × 19cm) rectangle. Sew along the three open sides, leaving a turning gap in the long side. Turn to the right side, using a wooden stick or similar to push out the corners, then iron. Topstitch along the long folded edge.

6 Centre the pocket and topstitch it to one of the finished lining panels, topstitching the turning hole closed at the same time. Run another line of stitching down the centre of the pocket to divide it into two compartments.

7 Fuse fusible fleece to each outer tote panel following the manufacturer's instructions, then quilt the outer panels, as desired.

8 Place the outer panels right sides together and sew along the bottom and sides. Repeat for the lining panels, leaving a 4–5in (10–13cm) opening in the bottom.

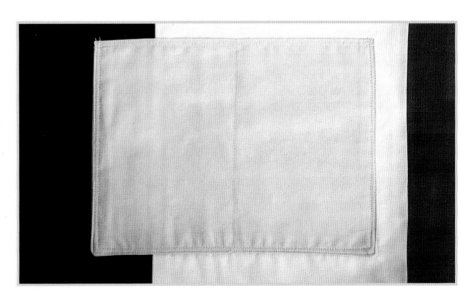

9 To form the boxed corners, take the outer tote piece (wrong sides out) and match the side and bottom seams at one corner. Hold flat, centre the seam, and measure 2½in (6.5cm) up from the point. Draw a line across from side to side. Sew along the line and trim the seam to ½in (1.2cm). Repeat with the other corner and both corners of the lining.

10 To make the handles, fuse the interfacing to each 4 × 20in (10 × 50cm) handle rectangle, then fold them in half lengthways with right sides together. Sew along the open long sides and turn each handle right side

out. Iron and topstitch along each long side and then again ¼in (6mm) away from each long edge. Loop each handle over and centre on the tote so the raw edges are aligned (the loops should be pointing down). The inner edges of each handle loop should be spaced 4in (10cm) apart. Tack (baste) in place.

11 Turn the outer tote piece right side out and place inside the lining piece, right sides together. Align the side seams and pin, then sew along the top edge. Turn the tote right side out through the opening in the lining and stitch the turning gap closed. Finally, iron the top edge and topstitch around.

----SNUGGLE SOFT PLAYMAT----

Emily Levey

This adorable quilt playmat, featuring fun fabric prints and colourful ties, is ideal for baby's playtime. Use any backing of your choice: here I have chosen supersoft fleece for a soft and comfortable finish, perfect for snuggling beneath.

MATERIALS

- 6 fat quarters of fabric
- 37 × 54in (94 × 138cm) backing of your choice

◆ PATTERN NOTES
Seam allowance is ¼in (6mm), unless stated otherwise

Top Tip

TAKE CARE NOT TO STRETCH THE BACKING OUT OF SHAPE, PARTICULARLY IF YOU ARE USING FLEECE.

1 Cut nine 6in (15cm) squares from each fat quarter.

2 Lay out the 54 squares in your desired arrangement of six columns by nine rows. With right sides facing, stitch the squares in each row together. Iron the seam allowances on each row in opposite directions

3 Place the first two rows together with right sides facing. Align the seams, so they lock together with the seam allowances facing in opposite directions and sew, using a walking foot if you have one. Repeat until all rows are joined, then iron the seam allowances.

4 With the right side facing up, place the backing smoothly out onto a large, solid surface, securing the corners in place with masking tape if needed.

5 Place the completed quilt top down on the backing, right sides facing, ensuring there is an even overlap of backing fabric all the way around. Pin the layers together along all four edges.

6 Starting in the middle of one side, sew around with a ⅝in (1.5cm) seam allowance, stopping about 10in (25cm) short of the starting point to leave a turning gap. Reverse stitch at the start and end to secure the stitches.

7 Trim the bulk from the corners and excess backing and turn the quilt the right sides out. Push out the corners and gently iron along the seams to ensure they sit on the very edges of the quilt. Fold in the unsewn raw edges of the opening and iron, then pin together.

8 Topstitch around the quilt, ¼in (6mm) from the edge, to close up the opening.

9 Thread the needle with coordinating embroidery cotton and insert it through both layers of the playmat, coming back up ¼in (6mm) away. Leave a 2–3in (5–7.5cm) tail then repeat the stitch in the same location, this time pulling the thread taught.

10 Cut the thread, leaving another 2–3in (5–7.5cm) tail, then tie the two tails together with a double knot. Trim the tails to your desired length: around 1in (2.5cm) is best.

11 Repeat Steps 9–10 over the rest of the playmat using embroidery cotton in different colours; this one is tied at the corner of every block.

Top Tip

IF YOU ARE USING FLEECE BACKING, MAKE SURE THE IRON IS NOT TOO HOT WHEN PRESSING THE SEAMS.

COUNTRY CONTRAST PILLOW

Jessie Fincham

This 15in (38cm) square pillow is the perfect addition to a country cosy living room or bedroom. The half square triangles that form the pattern are so simple to make. Play with the contrast of colour and pattern within each square for striking results.

MATERIALS

- 7 fat quarters of fabric: 5 for pillow top (plain beige, blue check, cream floral, plain green, purple floral), 2 for pillow back

1 Cut two 3in (7.5cm) strips from the width of fabric from the beige, check and cream fat quarters, then sub-cut each fabric into nine 3in (7.5cm) squares. Cut one 3in (7.5cm) strip from the width of fabric from the green and purple fat quarters, then subcut each fabric into five 3in (7.5cm) squares.

2 To make a half square triangle (HST) place two 3in (7.5cm) squares right sides together. Draw a pencil mark through the diagonal and sew ¼in (6mm) from each side of the drawn line. Cut down the centre line to yield two HST units and iron towards the darker side.

3 Repeat with 18 squares, using your chosen fabric placement, to yield a total of 36 completed HST units. Sew the blocks together as shown and iron the seams open.

4 Join the pillow top in rows, carefully matching the correct fabric placement. Iron the seams to the side, alternating with each row so the seams can 'nest' together.

5 Cut two 15½ x 11½in (39.5 x 29cm) pieces from the backing fabric. Fold the shorter side over by 1in (2.5cm) and again by 1in (2.5cm), enclosing the raw edge, and iron. Sew ⅛in (3mm) from the folded edge. Repeat for the other side.

6 With right sides together, place the pillow top with the pillow sides on top of each other. Pin and sew ¼in (6mm) around the edge. Cut the corners and trim off the excess with pinking shears.

----PEEK-A-BOO HOUSE HANGING----

Prudence Rogers

This home-sweet-home wall hanging is perfect for a nursery or child's bedroom. Little ones will have great fun opening the flaps and exploring the textures and pictures. Add your own photo in the plastic pocket and change it regularly for a new surprise every time.

MATERIALS

- ◆ 7 fat quarters: 2 plain off-white fabric, 5 patterned print fabric in different colours
- ◆ 3¼in (8cm) square clear PVC plastic
- ◆ 3¼in (8cm) diameter circle of plastic mirror sheet
- ◆ ⅝in (1.6cm) wide bias binding: 2yd (1.8m) length of turquoise, 30in (75cm) length of pale pink
- ◆ 20in (50cm) medium weight wadding (batting)
- ◆ 10in (25cm) featherlite iron-on adhesive
- ◆ ¾in (2cm) plastic ring

1 Square up one of the plain fat quarters and cut an 18 × 21¼in (46 × 54.5cm) rectangle. Fold in half lengthways and measure 9in (23cm) down from the top on the raw edge. Cut diagonally through both layers of fabric from the fold on the top edge to this mark. Open out to create the house shape.

2 To make the flaps, cut a 5 × 10¼in (13 × 26cm) rectangle from one of the patterned fabrics and fold in half with right sides together to make a square. Sew around the three open edges using a ¼in (6mm) seam allowance, leaving a 2in (5cm) opening on the side opposite the fold. Clip the corners and turn right sides out. Tuck in the raw edges of the opening and iron flat. Topstitch around three sides, ¼in (6mm) from the edge, leaving the side with the opening. Make another flap of the same size in a different patterned fabric then, using the same technique, make two more flaps by cutting two 10¼ × 10½in (26 × 27cm) pieces.

3 Position the flaps onto the house, 1⅛in (2.8cm) in from the sides with ¾in (2cm) between them, so the gaps are even and the flaps are straight. Mark the corners of each flap with disappearing marker and remove.

4 Mark out a triangle: 15in (38cm) wide by 7½in (19cm) tall at the central apex, onto the paper backing of the iron-on adhesive. Roughly cut out and iron onto the wrong side of the roof fabric, following the manufacturer's instructions. Neatly cut out the triangle and iron onto the roof area of the house fabric, leaving an equal border around the edges. Sew around the edges a couple of times using straight stitch and matching thread.

5 Position the plastic mirror circle in the centre of the space marked for one of the square flaps. Draw around and remove. Take a 13in (33cm) length of bias binding and fold one end under by ¼in (6mm) to hide the raw edge. Fold the end in half lengthways and, using the circle as a guide, sew to the house background. Sew close to the outside edge of the binding while folding and feeding around the circle as you go: the folded edge of the binding should be around the inner edge of the circle. Trim the binding at the end, leaving a ⅜in (1cm) overlap, then tuck the raw edge under and finish sewing down.

6 Remove any protective film from the plastic mirror, apply a small amount of glue to the back and tuck it under the binding, gradually easing it in all the way around.

7 Cut a 3½in (9cm) square of clear plastic and a 17in (43cm) strip of bias binding.

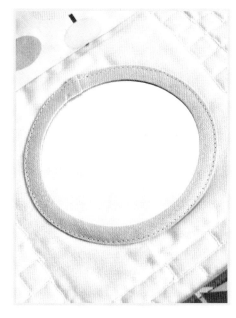

Top Tip

DON'T BE TOO PRECISE WITH THE
SIZE AND SHAPES OF YOUR BRICKS:
A RANDOM FORMATION HAS A CUTE
EFFECT. AVOID CATCHING THE EDGES
OF THE FLAPS IN YOUR STITCHING.

Fold the raw end of the binding under by ¼in (6mm) and iron. Starting with the folded end halfway along one of the edges of the plastic, pin around the edge, folding the binding in half lengthways and tucking the corners in as you go. Leave a ⅝in (1.5cm) overlap where the ends meet and turn under the raw edge. Tuck the two ends into one another and flatten to match the edges. Sew the binding around the plastic, close to the folded edge. Pin to the background fabric where the bottom right square flap will be placed and sew around three sides, leaving the top of the pocket open on the inner edge of the binding (see Fig 1).

8 Using the templates (see Templates) mark out two lovebirds (flipping the template for one so you have a mirror image), two hearts and two wings (again making one a mirror image) on the paper backing of the appliqué adhesive. Cut out roughly. Choose parts of the fabrics that complement the appliqué shapes, then iron and cut out neatly. Iron to adhere the appliqué to the background fabric in the space under one of the long flaps, copying the arrangement shown. Free-motion

stitch around the edges of the designs to add details, such as the legs and beaks.

9 Repeat Step 7 with the flower and flower centre templates, stitching in the space left for the other large rectangular flap.

10 Pin all the flaps into position and sew along the tops, reverse stitching at each end.

11 Cut a piece of wadding and backing fabric, both 5cm (2in) larger around than the house shape. Place the plain backing fabric wrong side up, sandwich the wadding in the centre and lay the house piece right side up on top. Insert small safety pins, about 10cm (4in) apart, all around through the three layers.

12 Using matching thread, free-motion quilt the roof fabric in a tile pattern using rows of joined 'U' shapes (see Fig 2). Straight stitch up and down the backing fabric at the sides of the roof using white thread.

13 Fill in the rest of the background fabric using brick-effect free motion quilting with white thread, forming the brick pattern with overlapping rectangles. Trim the backing fabric and wadding to the same size as the front.

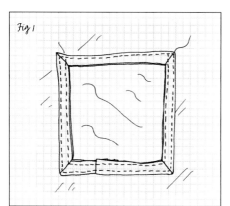

Fig 1

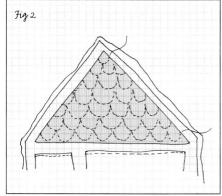

Fig 2

14 To bind the finished hanging, use a 66in (1.8m) length of ready-made bias binding. Open it out and pin the opened edge level with the edge of the hanging, wrong sides together, all the way around the house shape. For the corners, fold the binding at 90 degrees to itself to create a triangle, then fold back in along the edge of the quilt. Leave 2–3in (5–7.5cm) overlapping at the join before cutting the binding (see Fig 3).

15 Start sewing in the crease of the bias binding, leaving the first 5cm (2in) to allow for joining at the other end. At the corners, lift the triangular flap up vertically one way and then the other, so it is not trapped in the seam. Leave a further 5cm (2in) free at the end of the binding. To join, lay the two binding ends on top of each other and mark where they meet. Now lay them at right angles to

each other, lining up the marks with right sides together. Pin across the two strips on the diagonal, then open out to check the length. If the binding fits, sew across the diagonal and trim the remaining strips to leave a ¼in (6mm) seam (see Fig 4). Now finish sewing to the hanging.

16 Turn over the binding, wrapping in the edges of the hanging and bringing it to the front, covering the stitching you just made. Iron, flattening out the corners so that they are mitred, and pin into place. From the right side, sew close to the edge of the binding all the way around. Finally, hand sew a plastic ring to the back for hanging.

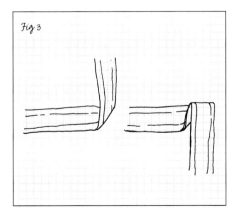

Fig 3

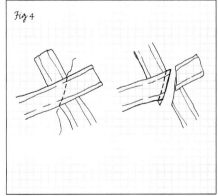

Fig 4

----GARDEN PARTY TABLECLOTH----

Liz Betts

Add a splash of colour to your dining room or garden table with this stripy patchwork tablecloth in two contrasting colourways. Finish it in no time by simply leaving the back open or back with fabric for a heavier, more durable tablecloth, suitable for outside events.

MATERIALS

- 9 fat quarters of fabric: 5 in one colourway, 4 in another
- 1½yd (1.4m) square of backing fabric (optional)

1 Take the set of four fat quarters and cut each one to measure 17½ × 19½in (44.5 × 49.5cm). Now cut each piece into three strips measuring 17½ × 6½in (44.5 × 16.5cm).

2 Make four piles from the strips, each containing three pieces of fabric. Shuffle the colours and prints so that each pile contains different fabrics.

3 Take the first pile. Sew the three strips together along the 17½in (44.5cm) side,

using a ½in (1.2cm) seam allowance, to make a 17½in (44.5cm) square. If needed, pin each end of the fabric to make sure both ends line up and don't stretch. Iron the seams open and repeat with the other three piles.

4 Repeat Steps 1–3 for the remaining five fat quarters, making piles from the fabrics and sewing them together to make five squares.

5 Lay out the squares to make a 3 × 3 arrangement (see Fig 1). Stitch together to make three rows, using a ½in (1.2cm) seam allowance. Iron, then sew the rows together.

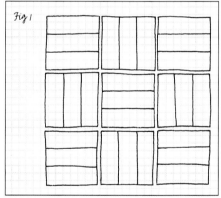

Fig 1

6 If you are not backing the tablecloth with fabric, the seams need to be neatened using pinking sheers, zigzag stitch or overlocking to prevent fraying. Fold and iron a ½in (1.2cm) hem all the way around the tablecloth and stitch into place.

7 If you are backing the tablecloth, iron the backing fabric square and lay it out, then place the tablecloth centrally on top and pin the layers together. The layers need some stitching through them to prevent them from 'bagging'. I stitched four horizontal lines, each ½in (1.2cm) away from the seam line between the three rows, however you can sew any design you wish.

8 Cut the backing fabric 1in (2.5cm) wider than the tablecloth all around. On two opposite sides, fold the raw edge of the backing fabric level with the edge of the tablecloth. Iron, and then fold the sides over level to the edge of the tablecloth to create a hem. Pin and then stitch using matching thread. Repeat for the remaining two sides.

----QUICK BOHO QUILT----

Ali Burdon

This bright and beautiful quilt created from ten fat quarters is surprisingly quick and easy to complete. Cut squares of colourful coordinating fabrics from a card template and use the photograph as a guide to form your pattern, then the sewing can begin!

MATERIALS

- 10 coordinating fat quarters of fabric
- 52 × 70in (1.3 × 1.8m) piece of wadding (batting), suitable to be quilted up to 8–10in (20–25cm) apart
- 108 × 44in (2.75 × 1.1m) piece of backing fabric
- 9 × 10½in (23 × 27cm) card template

◆ PATTERN NOTES
Seam allowance is ¼in (6mm)

1 Using the card template, cut four 9 × 10½in (23 × 27cm) rectangles from each fat quarter. The short edge of the template should be placed parallel with the selvedge when cutting the pieces.

2 On a large flat surface, arrange the rectangles into five columns and eight rows, with the short edges running from top to bottom. Decide which prints will be fabrics A – J, then arrange the rectangles (see Fig 1). Place the pieces from each column into separate piles, so you have five piles of eight rectangles.

3 Sew each set of eight pieces together along the long sides to make five columns. Label each column 1– 5 as you complete it. Iron all the seams open.

4 Stitch the five columns together along the long edges and iron the seams open.

5 Cut a piece of backing fabric measuring 52in (1.3m) × the full width of fabric and two pieces measuring 14 × 52in (35.5 × 130cm) and trim any selvedges. Matching the 52in (1.3m) edges, stitch the two smaller pieces onto either side of the large piece to create a rectangle. Iron the two seams open. Fold the backing in half, right sides together, bringing the two short sides together and put aside.

6 Place the wadding on a large flat surface with the completed quilt on top, right side up. Smooth it out. Working from the centre out, pin the wadding and quilt top together, placing quilting safety pins at every seam intersection and in the centre of each block.

Fig 1

H	F	D	B	J
G	E	C	A	I
F	D	B	J	H
E	C	A	I	G
D	B	J	H	F
C	A	I	G	E
B	J	H	F	D
A	I	G	E	C

Top Tip
IT'S A GOOD IDEA TO TAKE A PICTURE OR MAKE A NOTE OF YOUR LAYOUT TO USE AS A REFERENCE.

7 Place the folded backing on the quilt top, lining up the fold with the central seam. Carefully unfold the backing, keeping the fold line aligned with the central seam so the backing and quilt top are right sides together. Smooth out the backing and pin it in place around the edges of the quilt top, inserting ordinary pins parallel with the edges. The backing will overlap, but it is easier not to trim it at this stage.

8 Carefully roll up the quilt. Working on the wadding side, machine stitch around the edge with a generous ¼in (6mm) seam allowance. Ensure that your work surface supports the weight of the quilt as much as possible. Start stitching in the middle of one of the short edges and stop about 18in (46cm) from where you started. Reverse stitch at the

beginning and end of your stitching and remove the pins as you sew.

9 Trim off the excess backing fabric and turn right side out, pushing out the corners with a wooden stick or similar. Gently iron the seam edge. Turn the raw edges of the turning gap in and either hand stitch closed with ladder stitch or use pins or washable glue to hold the fabric together temporarily. Topstitch the edge of the quilt.

10 Working with the quilt top facing you and using an 18in (46cm) length of perle cotton and a large-eyed needle, find one of the seam intersections towards the middle of the quilt and take the needle down through all three quilt layers, just to one side of the intersection. Bring the needle back up ¼in (6mm) away, leaving a 2in (5cm) tail. Repeat once more in the same place, leaving another 2in (5cm) tail. Tie the two thread ends in a double knot, then trim the ends to about 1in (2.5cm). Tie similar knots at every seam intersection and in the middle of each block to finish.

Top Tip

ENSURE THAT YOU HAVE PLENTY OF TABLE SPACE AVAILABLE ON THE LEFT SIDE OF YOUR SEWING MACHINE TO SUPPORT THE QUILT AS IT GETS LARGER.

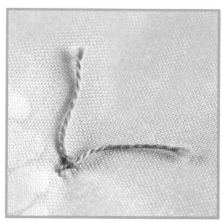

----DOUBLE-SIDED STAR PILLOW----

Kaye Prince

This large, comfortable floor pillow features a striking star pattern made up from half square triangles in plain and patterned fabrics. Turn the cushion over for a repeat of the design in an alternative colourway, or leave this side plain for a quicker make.

MATERIALS

- ◆ 10 fat quarters of fabric:
  8 print, 2 solid
- ◆ 1¼yd (1.1m) square of quilt wadding (batting)

◆ PATTERN NOTES
Seam allowance is ¼in (6mm)

1 Cut four 6in (15cm) squares each from one print and one solid fat quarter. Cut four 5½in (14cm) squares from print fabric and two 6in (15cm) squares from solid fabric. Now cut one 6in (15cm) square and one 5½in (14cm) square each from two print fat quarters and eight 5½in (14cm) squares from one print fat quarter.

2 Repeat Step 1 for the five fat quarters that make up the reverse of the pillow. Then cut two 30in (75cm) squares from quilt wadding.

3 Make the half square triangles by matching up all 6in (15cm) squares in pairs of one solid and one print square. Draw a diagonal line from corner to corner on the back of one square, then match squares with right sides together and pin. Sew a line ¼in (6mm) from each side of the drawn line. Cut the square in half along the drawn line and iron each half open. If necessary, trim the square down to 5½in (14cm). Repeat for each 6in (15cm) square.

4 Lay out all the half square triangles and remaining squares, as shown in Fig 1. Sew all the squares together in each row then sew the rows together. At each corner, trim the corner square on the diagonal using the points of the two adjacent squares as a guide.

5 Repeat Steps 3 and 4 for the reverse side of the pillow.

6 Place one piece on top of the wadding and trim the wadding down to match the outline of the pillow. Repeat with the reverse of the pillow.

7 Tack (baste) each pillow piece to its respective wadding piece. If desired, quilt each pillow piece. Match the pillow pieces, right sides together, and sew along all sides using a ½in (1.2cm) seam, leaving a turning gap. Turn the pillow right sides out, using a wooden stick or similar to push out the corners. Stuff to the desired firmness and hand sew the turning gap closed.

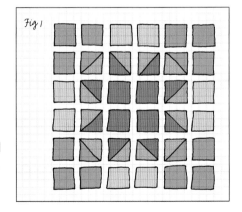

Fig 1

CELEBRATION TABLE RUNNER

Jo Avery

This special table runner is the perfect centrepiece for both a summer garden party and a festive celebration! Cut and piece together fabrics to create a winter street, complete with Christmas tree and wreaths, then turn over for a fun, bunting-adorned summer scene.

MATERIALS

- 10 fat quarters of fabric: 2 stripe, 1 pink, 1 blue, 1 turquoise, 2 charcoal, 1 white, 1 red, 1 green
- 2 pieces of muslin or old sheeting measuring 14 × 64in (35.5 × 162.5cm)
- Scraps of coloured felt and embroidery

◆ PATTERN NOTES

Seam allowance is ¼in (6mm), unless stated otherwise. Try to iron all seams towards the darker side of the fabric. The house blocks will be strip pieced (trimmed to size after they are sewn). Your fat quarter will have one side slightly shorter/longer than the other; follow the instructions given for where it is important to cut from a certain side.

1 Cut the following from the fat quarters:
CHARCOAL 1 (long side): one 3½in (9cm) strip for windows – cut into six 3½in (9cm) squares, three 2½in (6.5cm) strips and a 1½in (4cm) strip. From the remainder cut two 5⅞in (14.75cm) squares.
CHARCOAL 2 (short side): cut three 1½in (4cm) strips, three 2½in (6.5cm) strips and from the remainder cut four 4⅞in (12.25cm) squares.

RED (long side): two 1½in (4cm), two 2in (5cm), one 3in (7.5cm), one 2½in (6.5cm) and one 3½in (9cm) strips – cut into two 3½ × 6½in (9 × 16.5cm) rectangles for the doors.

GREEN (long side): one 1½in (4cm), two 2in (5cm), one 2½in (6.5cm), one 3in (7.5cm) and one 3½in (9cm) strips – cut into two 3½ × 6½in (9 × 16.5cm) rectangles for the doors.

WHITE (long side): one 3½in (9cm) strip for windows – cut into six 3½in (9cm) squares. From the remainder cut two 5⅞in (14.75cm) and four 4⅞in (12.25cm) squares, and two 6⅜ × 5½in (16.5 × 14cm) and two 1⅜ × 4½in (3.5 × 11.5cm) rectangles.

STRIPE 1 (short side): three 2½in (6.5cm), one 1½in (4cm) and two 2½in (6.5cm) strips. From the remainder cut two 5⅞in (14.75cm) squares.

STRIPE 2 (long side): three 1½in (4cm) and two 2½in (6.5cm) strips. From the remainder cut two 4⅞in (12.25cm) squares.

BLUE: one 3in (7.5cm), one 2½in (6.5cm), one 1½in (4cm) and one 4⅜in (11.25cm) strips – from this cut one 4⅜ × 4¼in (11.25 × 11cm) piece – and from the remainder cut a 2½in (6.5cm) strip and a 1½in (4cm) strip. From the remainder cut 4⅞in (12.25cm) and 5⅞in (14.75cm) strips and a 6⅜ × 5½in (16.5 × 14cm) rectangle.

PINK: 3in (7.5cm), 2½in (6.5cm), 2in (5cm), 1½in (4cm), 3½in (9cm) strips – cut into six 3½in (9cm) squares for doors. From the remainder cut a 4⅞in (12.25cm) square.

TURQUOISE: 2in (5cm), 1½in (4cm) and 4⅜in (11.25cm) strips – from this cut one 4⅜ × 4½in (11.25 × 11.5cm) and one 3½ × 6½in (9 × 16.5cm) rectangle for the doors. From the remainder cut one 5⅞in (14.75cm) and one 4⅞in (12.25cm) square, and one 6⅜ × 5½in (16.5 × 14cm) rectangle.

2 Assemble your blocks, starting with the winter side of the table runner. For House 1 (first left on the runner) sew a 2½in (6.5cm) red strip to the top and bottom of a 3½in (9cm) square charcoal window, trimming to size. Sew a 1½in (4cm) red strip to the left of the unit and a 2in (5cm) red strip to the right. Repeat with a second window. Sew a 1½in (4cm) red strip to the top of a green door then sew the three units together and add a 1½in (4cm) charcoal strip at either side (see Fig 1).

3 Cut both 5⅞in (14.75cm) charcoal squares in half diagonally and repeat with the 5⅞in (14.75cm) white square. Sew a white triangle to a charcoal triangle to make a square. Repeat with the other white triangle, using triangles from the other charcoal square so the stripes run in the same direction. Put the other triangles aside for the second block. Sew these diagonal units to either side of a large white rectangle to form the roof and sew this unit to the house. Take a 2½in (6.5cm) charcoal strip and cut into a 9in (23cm) and a 6½in (16.5cm) piece. Sandwich a 2in (5cm) green strip between the charcoal strips as a chimney (see Fig 2).

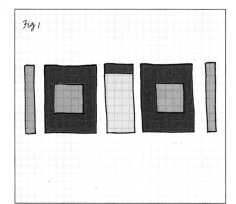

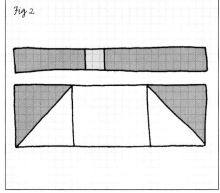

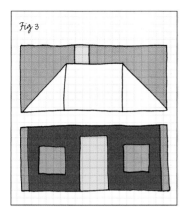

Fig 3

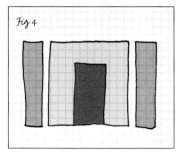

Fig 4

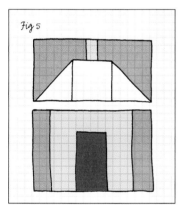

Fig 5

4 Sew the chimney strip to the top of the roof and the roof to the house (see Fig 3). Repeat Steps 2–3 for House 4, this time using a green house, a red door and a red chimney.

5 To make House 2, sew a 2½in (6.5cm) green strip above a red door, sew a 3in (7.5cm) green strip either side and sew a 2½in (6.5cm) charcoal strip to the left and right (see Fig 4).

6 Cut two 4⅞in (12.25cm) charcoal squares in half diagonally and repeat with the 4⅞in (12.25cm) white square. Sew a white triangle to a charcoal triangle. Repeat with the other white triangle, using triangles from the other charcoal square so the stripes run in the same direction. Put the other triangles aside for a second block. Sew these diagonal units to either side of a large white square to form the roof. Cut a 2½in (6.5cm) charcoal strip into two 6in (15cm) strips. Sandwich a 1½in (4cm) green strip between the two strips as a chimney. Sew the chimney strip to the top of the roof and the roof to the house (see Fig 5).

7 Repeat Steps 5–6 for House 5 using a red house, a green door and a green chimney.

8 To make House 3, sew 2in (5cm) red strips to either side of two charcoal windows. Sew a 1½in (4cm) red strip at the top and bottom of these units (see Fig 6) and add a 1½in (4cm) charcoal strip at either side.

9 Cut two 4⅞in (12.25cm) charcoal squares in half diagonally and repeat with the 4⅞in (12.25cm) white square. Sew a white triangle to a charcoal triangle and repeat with the other white triangle, using triangles from other charcoal square so the stripes run in the same direction. Put the other triangles aside for the second block and sew the roof together. Sew a 1½in (4cm) charcoal strip to the top and the roof to the house (see Fig 7).

10 Sew the five house blocks together. Sew a 2½in (6.5cm) charcoal strip at each end (see Fig 8).

11 Following Fig 9 and the steps for making up the winter houses (Steps 2–10), sew together five summer house blocks.

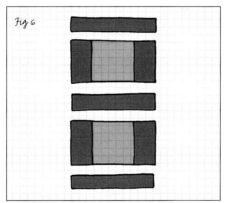

Fig 6

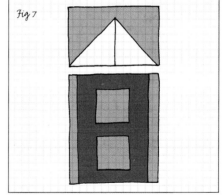

Fig 7

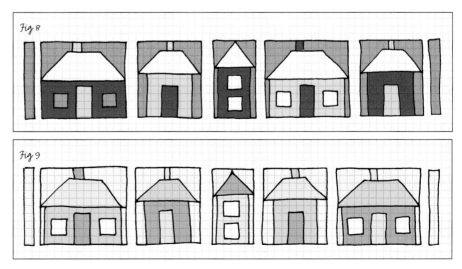

Fig 8

Fig 9

12 Place the completed winter side on top of one of the muslin/sheeting pieces, iron and attach some safety pins to hold together. Repeat with the summer side.

13 To embellish the winter side cut two wreath embellishments (see Templates) from green felt and pin to two doors. Cut a Christmas tree (see Templates) from green felt and pin to the window of the middle house. Using matching thread, neatly stitch the felt to the runner.

14 Embroider fairy lights and baubles onto the tree using backstitch, cross stitches and bullion knots.

15 Embroider your wreaths with lazy daisies, French knots and stars. Then embroider some more fairy lights in the windows of one of the other houses.

16 To embellish the summer side, use removable pen or fine pencil to draw bunting lines between the houses. With black embroidery thread, sew a running stitch along this line. Using your bunting flag pattern (see Templates) cut out 34 flags from different coloured felt scraps and pin at equal spaces along the bunting line. Using matching thread neatly sew the felt to the runner.

17 With right sides together, pin through all four layers and sew around three edges, leaving one short edge open. Snip the corners, turn inside out and iron. Fold in the open edge to match the other three seams, then iron and pin shut. Sew around all four sides of the runner using a straight topstitch, close to the edge, and closing your opening at the same time.

----CHEVRON QUILT----

Emily Levey

This fun quilt is surprisingly simple to make using one simple half square triangle (HST) block that is repeated throughout. It is the clever light and dark print selection that forms the striking chevron pattern.

MATERIALS

- 10 fat quarters of fabric: 5 light prints, 5 dark prints
- 20in (50cm) length of 44in (110cm) wide cotton fabric for binding
- 48 × 64in (122 × 163cm) quilter's wadding (batting)
- 50 × 66in (127 × 168cm) backing of your choice

◆ PATTERN NOTES
Seam allowance is ¼in (6mm), unless stated otherwise

1 Cut four 9¾in (24.5cm) squares from each fat quarter.

2 On the reverse of each light print square use a fabric marker to draw a diagonal line from one corner to the other. Pair each light print square with a dark print square. With right sides facing, sew two lines of stitching on either side of the diagonal line, ¼in (6mm) away from it. Cut down the line to give you two units and iron the seam allowances towards the dark print.

3 Repeat Step 2 until you have sewn all the squares together and have 40 HST units.

4 Trim each of the HST units so that they are 9in (23cm) square, taking care to ensure that the seam line runs diagonally from one corner to another.

5 Arrange the HST units to form the chevrons, using 35 units in a layout of five columns by seven rows (see Fig 1). With right sides facing, stitch the squares together until each row is sewn. Iron the seam allowances on each row in opposite directions.

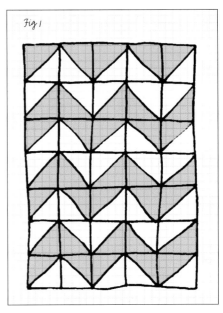

Fig 1

Top Tip

FOUR OF THE REMAINING FIVE HST UNITS CAN BE SAVED TO MAKE A COORDINATING CUSHION.

6 Place the first two rows together, right sides facing. Align the seams: they should lock together with the seam allowances facing in opposite directions, and sew. Repeat until all rows are joined and iron the seam allowances open to reduce bulk.

7 With the wrong side facing up, lay your backing out smoothly on a large solid surface, securing it in place with masking tape at the corners if needed. Take care not to stretch the backing out of shape.

8 Lay the wadding out smoothly on top of the backing. Place the completed quilt top on top

so the right side is facing up, ensuring that there is an even overlap of wadding/backing fabric all the way around. Pin through all the layers with safety pins, spacing the pins about 4in (10cm) apart around the quilt.

9 Quilt as desired. Here a straight stitch with a 1/8in (3.5mm) stitch length has been used to echo the zigzag lines of the chevrons. Remove the safety pins as necessary while quilting, then trim the excess backing and wadding once the quilting is complete.

10 Take your binding fabric and cut five 2½in (6.5cm) × width of fabric strips. Join the strips along the short ends so you have a long length. Iron the seam allowances open, then iron the binding in half lengthways to make a double fold binding. You will need your binding to be at least 6yd (5.5m) long.

11 On the front of the quilt and starting along the middle of one edge, leave around 6in (15cm) of the binding unsewn, and attach the binding to the quilt with a ¼in (6mm) seam allowance. Align the raw edges of the binding with the edge of the quilt. Mitre the corners as you go and stop sewing around 6in (15cm) from where you started.

12 Mark where the start of the binding tape overlaps with the tail end, then add on ¼in (6mm) for seam allowance and trim both ends. Join the short ends together using the ¼in (6mm) seam allowance, then finish attaching the binding to the quilt along the unsewn section. Hand stitch the binding to the reverse of the quilt to finish.

····STITCH LIBRARY····

The following stitches feature throughout the projects to add decoration, for hemming and for closing gaps and seams. See also the box feature for a description of the sewing machine stitches used in the book.

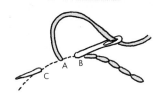

Backstitch

Backstitch is ideal for making a well-defined outline. Bring the needle out at A and take it to B to make a stitch. Now bring the needle back past the first stitch to C and repeat in this way.

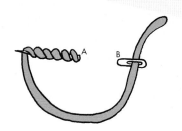

Bullion knots

Bullion knots are worked in a similar way to a French knot, but with more twists around the needle. Insert the needle at B and bring it out at A, without pulling it right through the fabric. Twist the thread around the needle five or six times, so the twists will cover the length between A and B. Place your thumb on the coiled thread and carefully pull the needle through to make the knot.

Ladder stitch

Ladder stitch is used to close a seam on a stuffed item or for sewing two folded edges together. Take straight stitches into the folded fabric, stitching into each edge in turn; the stitches look like a ladder. Pull the thread taut after a few stitches to close the seam.

Lazy daisy stitch

The lazy daisy stitch is a group of single, detached chain stitches worked in the shape of a flower. Bring the needle up through the fabric at the centre of the flower. Insert it again at the starting point and bring the tip up through the fabric at the opposite end, where the petal will end. Insert the needle back into the fabric on the opposite side of the thread, at the curved end of the loop, tacking it in place. Repeat to work additional stitches around the centre point.

Cross stitch

Cross stitch is worked to make decorative stitches. Bring the needle out at A and make a diagonal stitch to B. Now bring the needle out at C and make a second diagonal stitch to D. To make a row of cross stitches, bring the needle out at C again and repeat.

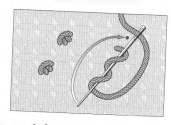

French knots

French knots can be worked singly as decorative stitches, in rows, or grouped together for a textured filling stitch. To make a French knot, bring the needle and thread through the fabric and wrap the thread around the needle three or four times. Holding this coil of thread in place, take the needle back through the fabric, just next to where it came out.

Straight stitch

Straight (long) stitch is worked like a single running stitch: you can make stitches of short or long lengths.

Tacking stitch

Tacking (basting) stitches are used to fasten layers of material together before stitching and can be removed once the stitching is complete.

 Stitches should be approximately ⅝in (1.5cm) long and evenly spaced.

Running stitch

This simple line stitch can be used to outline shapes or join two pieces of fabric together. Starting at the right-hand side, bring the needle out at A and insert it at B. Bring it out again at C and insert it at D. Continue in this way making sure the stitches and gaps are of even length.

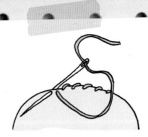

Slip stitch

Slip stitch is used to close gaps in seams. Work from right to left picking up a tiny piece of the fabric from one seam edge. Insert the needle into the other seam fold and move it along by ⅛in (3mm). Push the needle out and repeat.

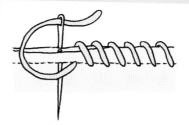

Whipstitch

Whipstitch (oversewing) is a simple stitch used to sew two pieces of material together. Pull each whipstitch tight for a neat finish.

Sewing machine stitches

FRENCH SEAM

In a French seam, the raw edges of the fabric are fully enclosed for a neat finish. First sew the seam with wrong sides together, then trim and iron the seam allowances. Next sew a second seam with right sides together, enclosing the raw edges of the original seam.

OVERLOCK STITCH

An overlock stitch connects two pieces of fabric with a series of thread loops that wrap around the outer edge of the material to prevent it from fraying. It can be used for hemming, reinforcement or decoration and is sometimes called serging, overedging, or merrowing. True overlock stitching requires an overlock machine, or serger.

STAY STITCH

Stay stitching is a simple row of stitches to help hold the shape of a piece of fabric. It is useful on diagonal cutting lines or curved areas, such as necklines, to prevent stretching. It can also be used for sewing over folds of fabric, such as tucks, to help to hold them in place.

TOPSTITCH

Topstitching is used most often on garment edges, such as necklines and hems, where it helps facings to stay in place and gives a crisp edge. It is generally done using a straight stitch with a matching thread.

ZIGZAG STITCH

A zigzag stitch is a back-and-forth stitch used where a straight stitch will not suffice, such as in reinforcing buttonholes, in stitching stretchable fabrics and in temporarily joining two work pieces edge-to-edge. When creating a zigzag stitch, a cam controls the back-and-forth motion of the sewing machine's needle. As the cam rotates, a finger-like follower connected to the needle bar rides along the cam and tracks its indentations. As the follower moves in and out, the needle bar is moved from side to side.

----TEMPLATES----

All templates are shown at 50 per cent; you will need to enlarge them by 200 per cent.
All of the full-sized patterns can be downloaded from http://ideas.stitchcraftcreate.co.uk/patterns

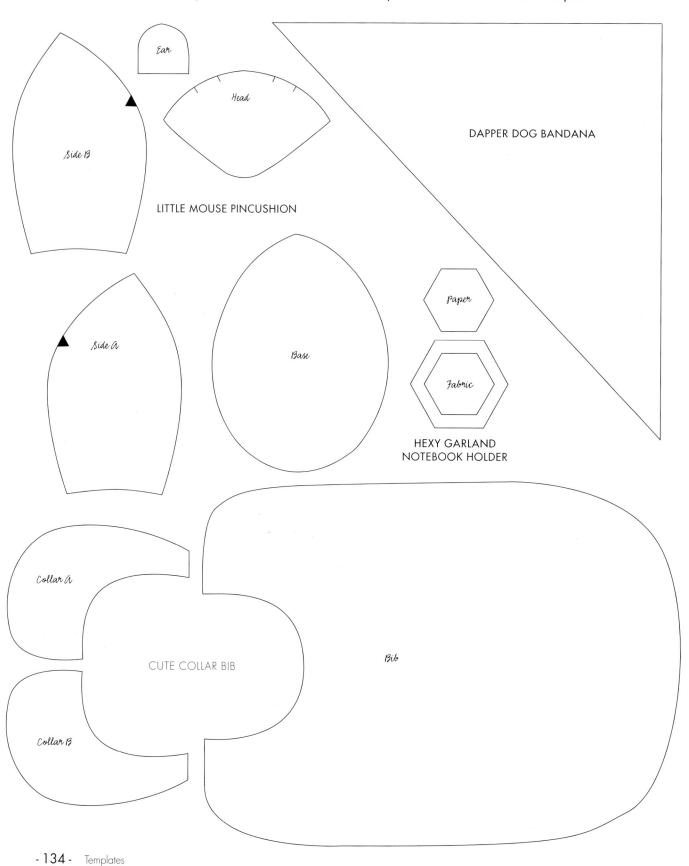

Ear

Head

Side B

DAPPER DOG BANDANA

LITTLE MOUSE PINCUSHION

Side A

Base

Paper

Fabric

HEXY GARLAND
NOTEBOOK HOLDER

Collar A

CUTE COLLAR BIB

Bib

Collar B

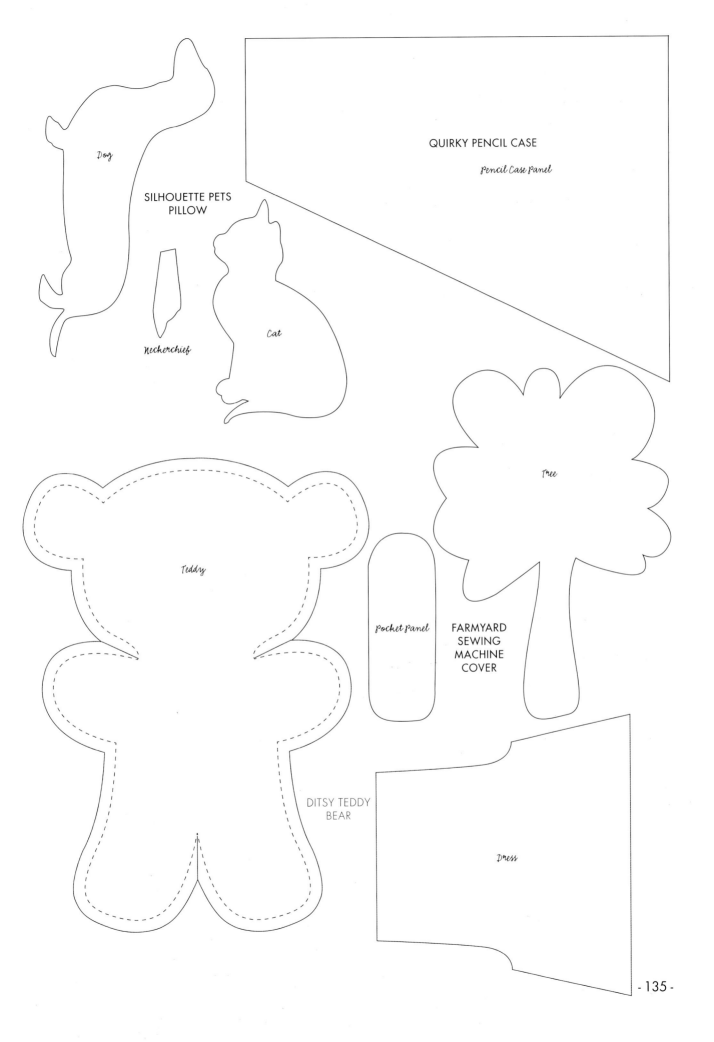

Dog

SILHOUETTE PETS
PILLOW

QUIRKY PENCIL CASE

Pencil Case Panel

Neckerchief

Cat

Tree

Teddy

Pocket Panel

FARMYARD
SEWING
MACHINE
COVER

DITSY TEDDY
BEAR

Dress

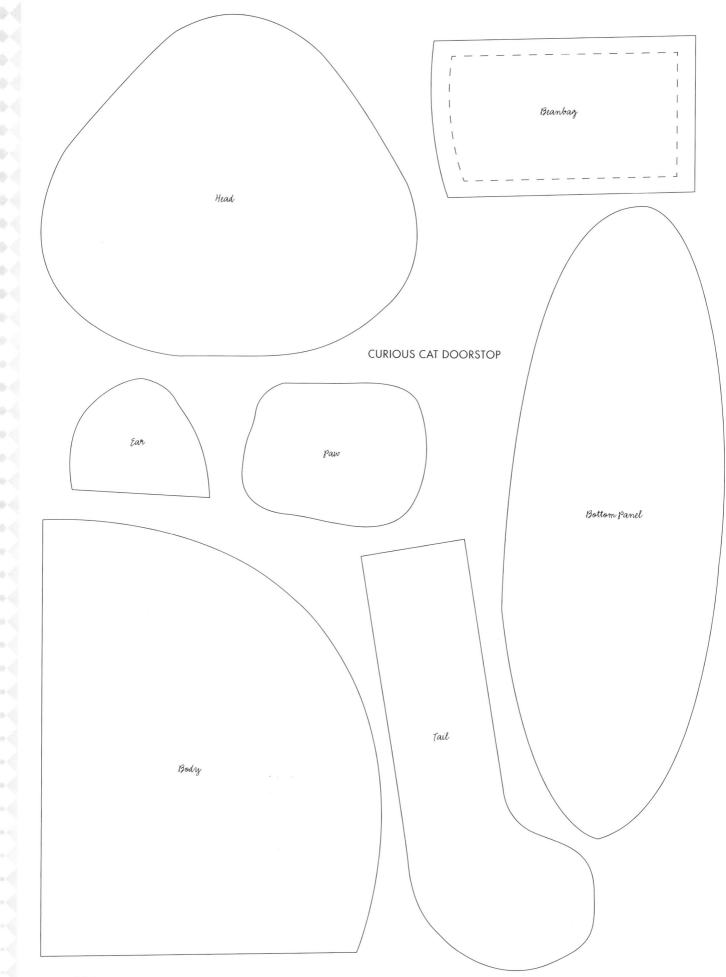

Head

Beanbag

CURIOUS CAT DOORSTOP

Ear

Paw

Bottom Panel

Body

Tail

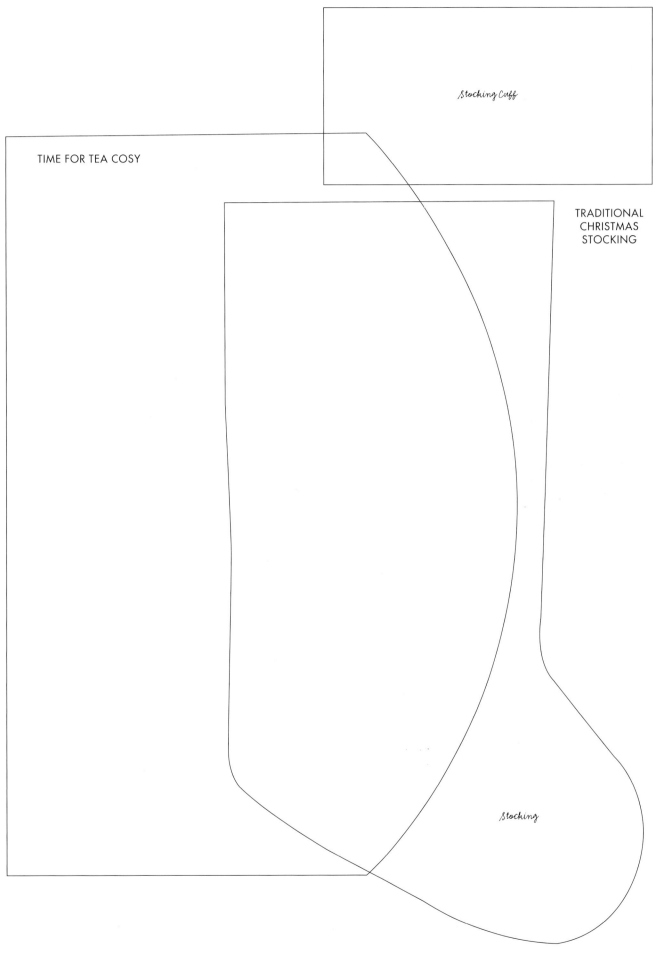

Stocking Cuff

TIME FOR TEA COSY

TRADITIONAL
CHRISTMAS
STOCKING

Stocking

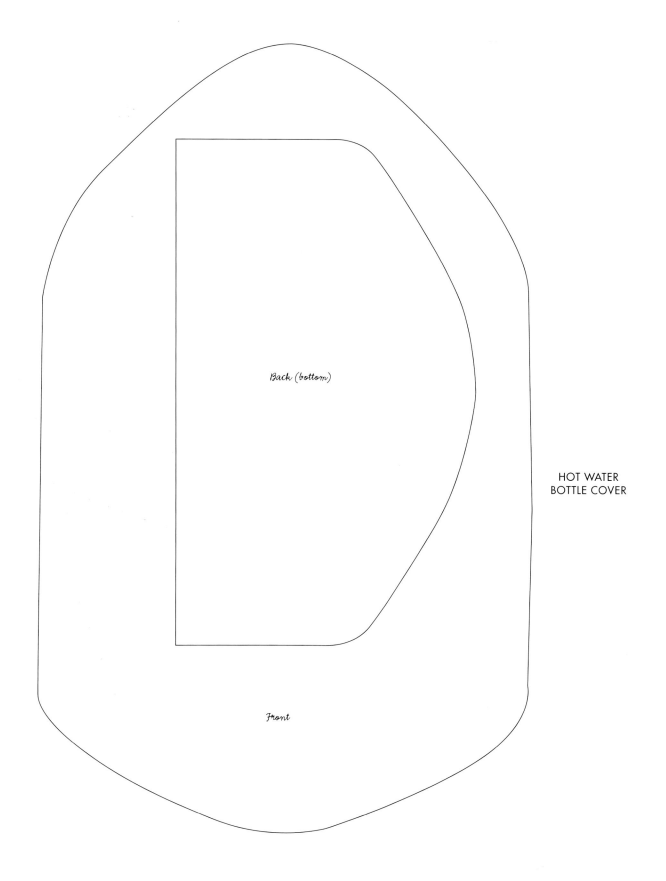

Back (bottom)

Front

HOT WATER
BOTTLE COVER

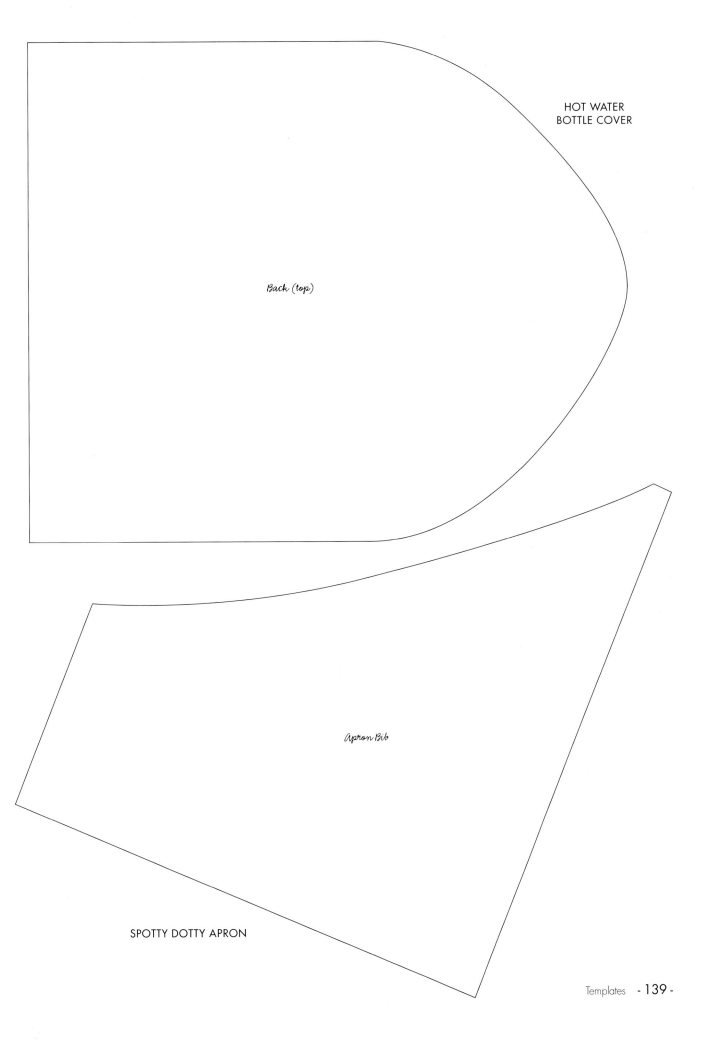

HOT WATER
BOTTLE COVER

Back (top)

Apron Bib

SPOTTY DOTTY APRON

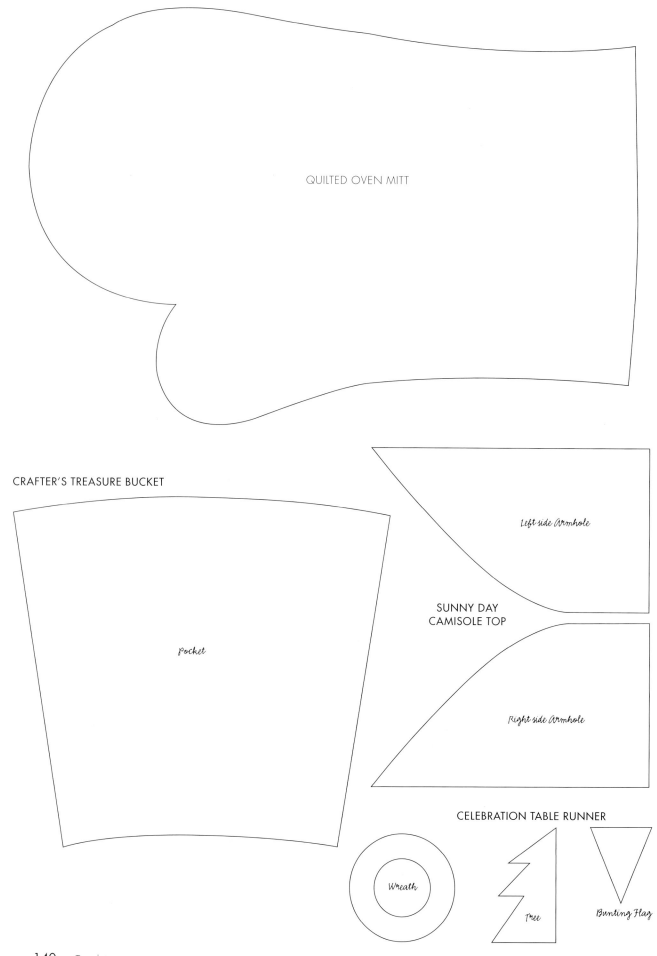

QUILTED OVEN MITT

CRAFTER'S TREASURE BUCKET

Pocket

Left side Armhole

SUNNY DAY
CAMISOLE TOP

Right side Armhole

CELEBRATION TABLE RUNNER

Wreath

Tree

Bunting Flag

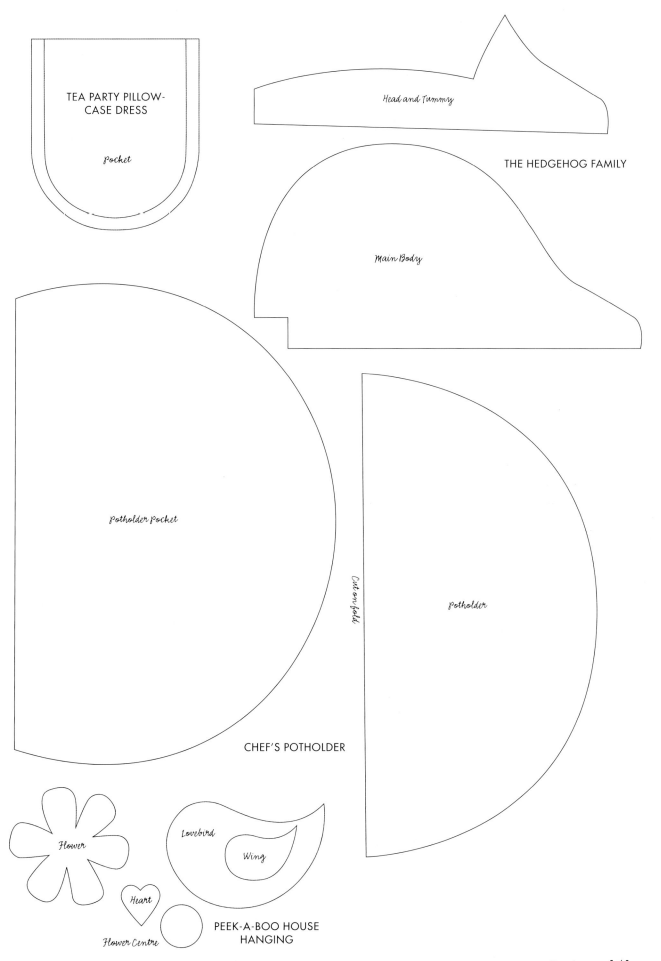

TEA PARTY PILLOW-
CASE DRESS

Pocket

Head and Tummy

THE HEDGEHOG FAMILY

Main Body

Potholder Pocket

Cut on fold

Potholder

CHEF'S POTHOLDER

Flower

Lovebird

Wing

Heart

Flower Centre

PEEK-A-BOO HOUSE
HANGING

--CONTRIBUTORS--

Jo Avery
www.mybearpaw.com

Liz Betts
www.quiltypleasures.co.uk

Ali Burdon
www.veryberryhandmade.co.uk

Jessie Fincham
www.messyjessecrafts.blogspot.co.uk

Lisa Fordham
www.etsy.com/shop/twinciehandmade

Louise Horler
www.sewscrumptious.blogspot.co.uk

Kevin Kosbab
www.feeddog.net

Emily Levey
www.strawberrypatchramblings.blogspot.co.uk

Kaye Prince
www.kayeprince.com

Prudence Rogers
www.instagram.com/PrudenceSays

Cynthia Shaffer
www.cynthiashaffer.typepad.com

The publishers would like to thank
all of the contributors whose designs
have been featured in this book.

--SUPPLIERS--

UK

Stitch Craft Create
www.stitchcraftcreate.co.uk

The Fat Quarters
www.thefatquarters.co.uk

US

Keepsake Quilting
www.keepsakequilting.com

JoAnn Fabric & Craft Stores
www.joann.com

Hobby Lobby Stores
www.hobbylobby.com

Checker Distributors
www.checkerdist.com

Brewer Quilting & Sewing Supplies
www.brewersewing.com

--INDEX--

A DAVID & CHARLES BOOK
© F&W Media International, Ltd 2015

David & Charles is an imprint of F&W Media International, Ltd
Brunel House, Forde Close, Newton Abbot, TQ12 4PU, UK

F&W Media International, Ltd is a subsidiary of F+W Media, Inc
10151 Carver Road, Suite #200, Blue Ash, OH 45242, USA

Text and Designs © F&W Media International, Ltd 2015
Layout and Photography © F&W Media International, Ltd 2015

First Published in the UK and USA in 2015

A catalogue record for this book is available from the British Library.

ISBN-13: 978-1-4463-0591-1 Paperback
ISBN-10: 1-4463-0591-0 Paperback

ISBN-13: 978-1-4463-7146-6 PDF
ISBN-10: 1-4463-71468 PDF

ISBN-13: 978-1-4463-7145-9 EPUB
ISBN-10: 1-4463-7145-X EPUB

Printed in China by RR Donnelley for:
F&W Media International, Ltd
Brunel House, Forde Close, Newton Abbot, TQ12 4PU, UK

10 9 8 7 6 5 4 3 2 1

Acquisitions Editor: Ame Verso
Editorial Manager: Honor Head
Desk Editor: Debbie Jackson
Project Editor: Bethany Dymond
Designer: Prudence Rogers
Photographer: Jack Kirby
Production Controller: Beverley Richardson

F+W Media publishes high quality books on a wide range of subjects.
For more great book ideas visit: www.stitchcraftcreate.co.uk

Layout of the digital edition of this book may vary depending
on reader hardware and display settings.